AARON

A TRUE DRUG STORY

I0103335

Aaron Phyall

chipmunkapublishing
the mental health publisher
empowering people

Aaron Phyall

Published by
Chipmunkapublishing
PO Box 6872
Brentwood
Essex CM13 1ZT
United Kingdom

http://www.chipmunkapublishing.com

Copyright © Aaron Phyall 2009
Printed in London England
First edition 2009

Chipmunkapublishing gratefully acknowledges the support of Arts Council England.

Aaron

CONTENTS

Aaron

Chapter 1 - *Extract from chapter 15* (Bangkok Nights)

It was New Years Eve 2003, I was in a restaurant on the banks of the Chao Phraya River in Bangkok. I was just finishing off a Gemology course and was spending a few days of the festive season with some friends I had made whilst living in the city.

The fireworks were going off and lights could be seen from all above, it was a truly beautiful sight. To this day I have never seen fireworks like this; the Thai's really know what they are doing when it comes to explosives. There were explosions that formed into planets of blue, red and green, shooting stars that shot across the sky and rockets that exploded into the night from the bridges, a spectacular sight.

The guys I was with were expatriates, John and Ralfi. They had retired to Bangkok on retirement visas. They had been living for some time in the city and really knew the score.

We were sitting at the table eating our Phat-Thai when the conversation turned to gemstones as it nearly always does, me being a Gemologist. I cannot remember exactly how the conversation went as it was a long time ago but we were talking about gold and the state of the world. I said that money was backed up by gold, as most of us are taught in school, John said "no its people!" "People" I said how can money be backed up by people? He went on to say that if all the money in the world was divided up evenly then everyone would have a dollar a day to live on. At first I couldn't get my head around what he was saying but many years later I did.

Aaron

Chapter 2-*Extract from chapter 19* (St. Martins)

Margate, England Winter 2005: There was a knock at the door, it was the police. My family and the doctors had decided I should be sectioned under the Mental Health Act for the second time. The police come into my room and stood there all intimidating, the way only police can do. Arms folded and feet at a stance they informed me I was to get my stuff and an Ambulance would be coming for me.

The Ambulance turned up with three paramedics all dressed in green, just like on the TV program Casualty. I can tell you now I did not want to go with them, the police made it quite clear I had to. I got my stuff together, toothpaste, clean clothes and put them in a bag. By this time I am scared out of my whits as I made my way down the stairs to the Ambulance with the crew and Police in tow.

Once in the Ambulance the crew assured me I would be okay, I was shaking like a leaf and scared out of my mind. It was a 40 minute drive to the mental facility in Canterbury, which was where they were taking me. I started to recollect the circumstances which had occurred and had led to all this happening.

Chapter 3 - The Beginning

St.Georges C of E School, Gravesend 1988. It was July and the last day of the summer term, I was in the sixth form and in the sixth form community area of the school. Everyone was in good spirits and some of us were in fancy-dress, there was a little bit of alcohol flowing as we all celebrated the fact that this was the last day of our school life. I walked out towards the toilets and met Erick on my way. Erick was new to the school and he had moved from Scotland with his mum and her new boyfriend. He was a tall skinny guy with blonde hair and stubble, a bit like shaggy from Scooby Doo, word had it he was a bit of a 'reckoner'. I'd seen him about in the past year but never really had too much to do with him as I tended to stay in with my close group of friends.

Erick greeted me with a big red face, slitty eyes and a big smile. I would know now what he had been up to but back then I was naive and knew nothing about drugs; I thought he had been drinking. He proceeded to follow me into the toilets where he pulled out a packet of Rizla and a small brown substance he called cannabis. He took three Rizla papers and stuck them together, two side by side on the ends and the other one overlapping them in the middle. I remembered being fascinated by what he was doing but also very nervous at the thought of being caught. He then proceeded to empty cigarette tobacco into his hand and burn the small brown substance with a lighter. A puff of smoke puffed up and a strong

Aaron

spicy smell filled the air. Then he sprinkled the cannabis into the tobacco and mixed it about a bit. The mixture was then made into a cigar shape on one hand, a small piece of Rizla card rolled up and put at one end. The Rizla papers were then placed on the other hand. He slapped his hands together and a couple of seconds later was presenting me with what he said was a 'joint'. I smoked it! I begun to feel all hot and the taste of the cannabis was so strong it wouldn't leave my mouth. A few minutes later I was sick everywhere, that was one of the few times I actually smoked a joint, this experience really put me off smoking cannabis but it didn't put me off importing and selling it. From this point, Erick would become my partner in crime for the next few years. I spent the rest of the summer buying ounces of cannabis and selling it.

Chapter 4 - Shetland Bound

After leaving School I had enrolled on an apprenticeship scheme as a Stonemason. Steven Lonsdale was the guy I was working for. I was at my banker (a banker being the table made of stone slabs we worked on) when my phone rang. I had made a few thousand quid so far from selling cannabis and bought one of the first true mobile phones, it was a Motorola brick phone. I answered the call, it was Erick.

I have a plan he said, I'm going back to Shetland for the winter and have a few mates that smoke, how would you like to bring some gear up and we could sell it. At that time I was rubbing the saw marks out on a piece of Portland stone, my fingers were blistering and I thought yes why not, I'm getting pissed off with this. Erick went up to Shetland that Christmas and we planned to meet up in the January in Lerwick, the main town in the Islands.

Christmas came and went and the time for me to leave was near. I got in contact with Terry, Terry was a lot older than us in his mid 30's, he used to be a hairdresser so he quickly got named Ter-rinse, he was our supplier. I arranged to meet in our usual place, Sun Lane just outside the Video shop. Just as I got there Terrinse turned up with a large holdall and handed it to me. That's a bit heavy I thought, expecting to be picking up about half a kilo, when he said Erick had phoned him and said he can sell loads and asked for 5 kilos. I

Aaron

remember thinking where am I going to put all that? I was going to get the train to Aberdeen then the boat as a foot passenger to Lerwick, I could never hide 5 kilos, I would have to take the car!

3am on the M6 and I was getting tired, I had only had my driving licence for little over a year and yet I found myself all the way up here on my own, where at every petrol station I stopped at the people spoke in funny accents. It was my first trip to Scotland and my first real drug adventure.

Morning came and I had been driving all night. I arrived at the port only to be told the crossing had been cancelled due to bad weather. I had to spend the night in Aberdeen so I set out to find the best hotel I could, after all I was now a drug smuggler, a fact that at the time I was quite proud of. I booked into the Tree Tops Hotel, a splendid place with a swimming pool, gym, Jacuzzi, a couple of restaurants and a mini bar! A high end Holiday Inn type place. I had never stayed in such luxury before and thought it was the best; I was only 18 at the time and used to camping and sleeping in my car.

I awoke midday to find the empty content of the mini bar thrown across the room; I had a hangover from hell! I got myself together and made my way down to the reception to pay the bill.

Before I left the car park of the hotel I decided to check the drugs before I got to the port. I had put the gear in the inside side panels of the rear of the car. Everything looked okay so I set of for the docks.

When I got there I was in luck the ship was sailing and the weather had calmed down. The ship left late afternoon so I had time to think about what I was doing. Was there a Customs at Lerwick? If so would they search the car? I hadn't really thought about this before and I must say I was beginning to get a bit nervous.

I drove onto the ship, the crossing would last about 13 hours. I had got a cabin to sleep in and I thought I would just sleep, this would then have the added advantage of me not thinking about things too much, I found my cabin and it consisted of 2 bunk beds. I put my rucksack with change of clothes on one of the top bunks and then instead of sleeping I decided to make for the bar!

The boat was full of lorry drivers taking their loads and collecting fish from the islands; we started to leave the port. The first half of the crossing was okay, a bit like a trip across the channel to France and I spent most of it propped up against the bar listening to stories from the lorry drivers. The waves then started, the boat was going up and down side to side and people were being sick all over the show; I only was just able to stop myself from being sick too. I went back to my cabin and tried to get some sleep.

I got out of my bunk the next morning with yet another hangover; the ship was pulling into the

Aaron

harbour so I got myself together and made my way to my car. The ramp went down at the front of the ship as I started my engine. I then proceeded to follow the traffic to disembark from the boat. Slight panic set in as I looked for police or some type of customs, there wasn't any, how relieved was I! Erick knew I would probably be on this sailing as I had phoned him from the hotel in Aberdeen as mobile phones didn't work in Scotland, it was still new technology.

I cannot quite remember where I met up with Erick but recall it was somewhere in the centre of Lerwick and probably a pub; Lerwick is a small place for a major town of the Outer Hebrides; I thought it would be a lot bigger. The town reminded me of small quaint villages in Cornwall where I had traveled to as a kid. There were buildings of stone, a small church and a winding high street splattered with a few pubs and restaurants; the sort of thing you see in old black and white photographs. I remember walking around the place and people were staring at me, it made me feel uneasy and a bit paranoid. It was later explained to me it was because I was a new face, something anyone from a village location would understand.

I met up with Erick okay and we made for the car. He explained he had found a place for me to stay with a scallop fisherman friend of his. We got in the car and proceeded to the place; it was about 20 minutes out of town. We crossed barren fields of grass and small hills of nothing; Shetland is not a nice looking place in the winter. We finally came to a house in a valley where a scrawny looking guy in his late 20's with a thick beard and long hair met us at the door. I forget his name but it was probably something Viking like Noose or Nor.

The next day another friend of Erick's met us at the house. I had already got the gear out of the car the following night when Viking man and Erick tried it; they said it was good shit! Viking man, Erick and his friend armed with a set of scales and a roll of cling film then proceeded to cut up and weigh the gear. I decided to go for a walk for a while whilst they did this; I didn't want to get my finger prints on this stuff I was thinking.

I returned about an hour later expecting them to be finished but instead there was a big pile of small pieces an eighth of an ounce in size; about 3.5 grams. They were cutting up the whole five kilos into Henrys; called Henrys because of Henry VIII, eighths being eighth of an ounce, 1428 pieces in total. I couldn't believe it! We ended up with a carrier bag full of Henrys. I was under the impression it was going to be sold in ounces. I remember thinking its going to take ages to sell all this; Viking man reckoned we had enough gear to supply all the islands for six months! Anyway once all this was completed Erick disappeared into the back garden with a spade and buried the lot.

I spent the next 2 weeks hanging out at the gym, going to the sauna and checking out what there was of the scenery. To tell you the truth it was relaxing at first but I soon got pissed off with it. There wasn't that much to do in Shetland for an 18 year old, I guess that's why they were all smoking 'dope'.

After a couple of weeks Erick admitted to me they were having trouble selling the gear. They had only sold a kilo and Terinse was promised his money within 4 weeks. Erick said I should leave him with another 285 Henrys and back the remaining 857 to Terinse! I laughed, I couldn't give him a carrier bag full of bits back he will go mad. After much thought I decided to give it a try as I didn't fancy spending the next few months sitting in Lerwick waiting for them to get ride of the rest of the gear.

I set off a couple days later with the 857 Henrys and about £4000 quid in Scottish money all tucked up safely in the side panels of the car. The trip on the ship on the way home was just as rough as the one coming, if not worse as we hit rough sea almost straight away. One of the guys sharing my cabin was accompanying his brother's body back to Aberdeen. He was a fisherman and had fell overboard, his brother said he was only in the water 10 minutes and when they got him out he was dead from hyperthermia. The North Sea is a crazy place in January.

Sun Lane video store, Gravesend. I was clutching my carrier bag wondering what Terinse would say about the state of the gear and the Scottish money. He pulled up on his mountain bike looking a bit puffed out as he was trying to lose weight due to over eating, a problem his brother Jason suffers from big time as well. I handed over the bag and he looked inside. I could tell by the look on his face he wasn't pleased. Terinse asked me if I could get rid of the gear, I said" I'd try". He took the money and left me with the stuff and pedaled off into the distance. I enlisted the help of my brother Burma and cousin Crowman and various friends in Higham and Isted Rise. Within a month or so it had all gone.

After returning from Shetland I went back to my apprenticeship at Stephen Lonsdale. I carried on selling gear after we had got rid of the Henrys but in quarter kilos, it was a lot easier and I only had to meet 5 or 6 people a week. Times were good I had money in my pocket, a nice car and was a bit of a face around town.

I had done about six months working as a stone mason and it was time to go to London to do the college half of the apprenticeship, this was something I was looking forward to. The college I was attending was really old, it was one of only two in the country and had been training stone masons for hundreds of years. It was located in Titchfield Street just of Oxford Street. My peers were a great bunch of guys and from all over the country, Kent, Wales, Newcastle and many other places. We had some great times in the classroom and around Soho and the rest of the city. The lecturers were really good to especially Charley Pucket, this man come out with some amazing

Aaron

stories.

Whilst walking from Oxford Street to the college I saw a book in the window of a shop that really caught my eye, I went in to look at it. It had a cloth cover which looked like papyrus and inside were pictures of tombs and the Pharaoh's of Egypt. One picture in particular caught my eye; it was a picture of the Tutankhamun burial mask. I bought the book and took it back to the college all excited, I was going to replicate the mask in Portland stone. I spent the next few weeks doing this much to the dismay of my tutor, we were meant to be making tracery windows. In the end I got a certificate for it and it was displayed in the reception for years. I continued to work for Steven Lonsdale but soon got fed up with rubbing the saw lines out on stone. I left the apprenticeship summer 1989.

Aaron Phyall

My copy of the Tutankhamun burial mask

My fascination continued after leaving college and
Stephen Lonsdale with Egypt, especially
Pyramids. A year or so later I got to travel there.

*I didn't realise the implications of how Egypt would
affect me and what I was to discover about the
world we live in and pyramids, until I found
Benjasiri Park (Queens Park) in Bangkok 15 years
later.*

Aaron

Chapter 5 - Rave On

My Granddad had discovered I was out of work. He was speaking to a friend of his Tosh who worked in London on the big construction sites. Tosh set up an interview for me with a company called Masonry Services in Deptford. I went to the interview and got the job, I was to do the pre-inspection fixing of all the granite work on their contracts at Canary Wharf. I was well chuffed!

I hadn't seen Erick for a while he had been getting into the rave scene in London, which was now becoming mainstream. Parties were going off every weekend all over the place in warehouses and fields; it had been like this for a year or so. I got a phone call from him and he asked me to come over sometime. I went out to his mum's house one Saturday morning and found him in bed. He had just got home on the milk train from London after spending the night out of his head on ecstasy. Ecstasy was something I had heard about but never tried and he knew this. He pulled out a bag full of white pills with doves printed on them "how much are they?" I asked, "25 quid" he replied. He suggested I come to a rave that night and try one "I'd have a great time and the feeling was amazing" he said. I was a bit hesitant as this was not cannabis but class A, I decided with a bit of persuasion to go. He also said he had met a guy who had some counterfeit money and was I interested, I thought about this for a while and said yes I'd have two grands worth. He said okay, he would sort it.

That night we arrived at Lea Bridge Road in London at a rave he called Dungeons. I remember attempting trying to park my car. There were people dancing in the street, cars in traffic jams with their boots open with music pumping out, it was utter chaos. We found a grass verge to park on, locked up the car and made for the entrance to the venue. There was a queue a quarter of a mile long to get into the place. Dungeons was situated under a bridge section of the Lea Bridge Road. We waited until we got to the front of the queue to pop our pills. Then we had to go through a security check, this was mainly to stop any competition from outside dealers from entering the place.

Once inside I could not believe what I was seeing, there were hundreds of people's heads bobbing up and down to this heavy base music. Their sweat was dripping off the brick tunnel ceiling and there was a mist of body heat filling the air. Erick pushed me to go on, people were just hugging each other and as I looked closer I noticed their jaws were grinding and jutting out. We walked through the main tunnel to an off shoot where it was a bit quieter. I looked around and there were sheets pinned up on the walls decorated in fluorescent paint. This was definitely like nothing I had ever seen or been to before.

We chatted for a while and Erick said hello to a few faces he knew from previous weekends. I started to feel a bit strange and tingly and could

Aaron

feel small rushes of what can only be described as feelings of wellbeing; my bottom jaw was moving around. I looked over at Erick and he was jumping around like a mad man and moving his arms up and down. I was out of it, my vision turned all blurry and my face was all warm. I started to move around to the music and found it added to the feeling I was getting from the drug. By this time the section we were in had filled up with people, everyone was jumping around going mental! I was starting to feel a bit paranoid; well this was a strange situation I was in. I jumped up and down all night until it was time to leave the place. When the music stopped everyone made their way to the exit, when we got outside it was light, I could not believe it someone said it was 10am!

I had a few more rave experiences in London but wasn't that keen on it as it was so new to me and I felt a bit conscious and paranoid. I did like ecstasy though and continued doing it every now and again over the years.

Mum's phone rang and I answered it "It's in the sand" a voice said, It was Erick. "What's in the sand" I said, "it's in the sand" Erick said. Erick didn't like saying too much on landlines he was a bit paranoid about being bugged, he was right to be so but it was hard trying to figure out what he was going on about half the time. He said he would be around in 10 minutes, the phone went dead.

There was a knock at the door, it was Erick "follow

me"he said and stormed through the house and down to the end of the garden. At the bottom we had a piece of land we called the allotment; I was building a workshop for my stone masonry on it. In the corner was a blue tarpaulin with sand under it, Erick steamed over to it and pulled the tarpaulin back. Under it was a massive amount of money, I then remembered the counterfeit "Oh, the counterfeit money is in the sand, Erick there's loads of it! "I said. He commented "well you asked for two grand's worth and that's two grand's worth! One thousand three hundred and thirty three tenners @ £1.50 is two grand! ". I hadn't asked how much they were per note when I ordered them! I went and got a carrier bag and put all the money inside, I was frightened it may get damp. I then took the bag in the house and we examined it. It looked really good although the paper was a little newish, too new; there was even water marks and a silver strip running down the middle. Erick left.

I wasn't sure where to put it so I put it in the tumble dryer until I could think of somewhere safe to keep it. That gave me an idea, I empted it out of the bag and turned the tumble dryer on and let it spin for a while on hot. This had the great effect of making the notes look a bit older. I must say I then did something more stupid than buying a load of counterfeit notes, I forgot to remove them from the tumble dryer after the cycle had finished. The next thing I knew was my Dad had come in from work and gone to put something in the tumble dryer, "what's this" he shouted. He then came into the

Aaron

front room of the house with a fist full of notes. He knew they were counterfeit as he worked for a Security Company picking up and delivering cash. It took me a few days to find out where he put the notes; I then promptly distributed them as soon as I found them, through my network of friends. I decided to keep a few back for a rainy day though.

I started my new job in Deptford and it was hard getting into it at first. I hadn't worked properly for quite a few months and was getting a bit lazy. My first day consisted of sand blasting a granite arch-way which had had mastic melted over it from a fire, this continued for the next week or so. I was the only English guy working in the yard, the rest were Portuguese masons. They were very skilled and could do amazing things with marble.

After my first few weeks of working I decided to visit a cousin of mine Jay on my way home. He was living in between the boarder of Greenwich and Deptford in a tower block. I didn't know him that well as he was a lot older than me and had lived in London most of his adult life, we didn't really mix as kids. I knocked at the door and he answered, he had long hair and a beard, a bit of a biker type dude and reminded me of Viking man from Shetland. He welcomed me in, I noticed he was smoking a joint and asked him if he wanted to sell some cannabis. He said yes and so we then started doing quite a bit of business around the Greenwich area.

I got in from work one day and read the local

paper, the 'Reporter'. There were articles on counterfeit money being received by shopkeepers all over the area. I knew that although it wasn't all down to me £13,000 is a lot of counterfeit and that's how much I had put out. I decided to get rid of the small stash I had left in Greenwich over the next few months.

That evening there was a phone call from my Auntie Betty (Jay and Crowman's mum) their house had just been raided by CID, they were looking for counterfeit money. I had given Crowman quite a bit of it to get rid of, thankfully he had shifted it all and they didn't find anything. She was just phoning Mum to tell her, little did she know the money had come from me, she would have gone mad if she had known as she thought the police had made a mistake.

It was approaching September and my 19th Birthday and Erick had been on the phone again speaking in his code. I couldn't get the full jest of what he was saying but something about organising a rave; we planned to meet up in a pub for a chat. When I arrived he was all excited and seemed to think the party scene was moving out of London and we could be the first to get involved in it in Kent. We put a plan together, Erick would organise the ecstasy and sound system and DJ's and I would sort the venue and logistics of the idea. He had been doing a lot of ecstasy lately and wasn't very organised and very paranoid. We planned to sell the tickets for £10 a pop and wanted somewhere that would hold 1000 people.

Aaron

I proceeded to look for a venue and must have visited all the farmers in the area looking for a barn or out buildings. Most of them had been watching the news and seen all the bad press on raves that were constantly on TV, I couldn't find anywhere they all said no. Then I remembered Clampin. Clampin was a friend from school who lived in a small village called Fairseat. This was a place near Meopham; I would go out and visit him sometimes. His family had a small holding and farm buildings; I would approach him with the idea.

I went to see Clampin and explained what we wanted to do. I said it was my birthday party and I needed a venue for the occasion. I had been advised if I made out it was my birthday party then the police couldn't stop it, also I thought it would go down better with Clampin's father. Clampin said they had no barns we could use but they had a field, the only thing is it needed cutting. Weeds were growing in it and the other farmers were getting pissed off because they were spreading to their fields. I said I would pay for the cutting of the field if they let me use it for my party, they agreed.

I had the venue, now all that was needed was a marquee and generator for the sound system. I scoured the yellow pages and with a mate Clive visited various suppliers to try and solve this, we found some. I asked an old school mate Stuart (one of the Wright brothers) to print the flyers and tickets for me, he did and they turned out tops.

The date of the rave came, it was during the day and I was waiting for the generator to arrive, some mates from Higham had already helped the marquee suppliers put the tent up, it looked impressive. Then a loud roaring came from down the lanes, it was the generator on the back of a 40 foot artic lorry, it was massive! We had to take a gate off to get the lorry in to the field. I was speaking to the lorry driver and he said he had just picked it up from a Bon Jovi concert in London, no wonder it was so expensive I remember thinking. Erick turned up late afternoon with the sound and lighting guys and drugs, someone had also ordered a big bouncy dragon though I cannot remember who! We had only sold about 150 tickets enough to cover our costs but were both hoping that the radio stations would give out our location and more people would come that night.

10 o'clock arrived and so did the DJ's, they started their sets and the music was loud; people started to arrive. Crowman was in charge of the car parking and I had friends on the gate taking tickets and cash. After about 1 hour into the DJ's set the police arrived"What are you doing here" I said to them, I was in my car near the gate and trying to answer my mobile phone at the time. "We heard the music from the station in Meopham and followed it" one of them replied. The station was about 7 miles away; apparently the sound and lighting people had used box speakers. This meant the sound was loud when you were close to the marquee but the further away you got the

Aaron

sound got even louder. We kept the whole village and half of Meopham awake most of the night. The police stopped it at about 3am, mainly because they put up road blocks to stop any more ravers getting in. It's a shame we didn't reach full capacity as we would have made a fortune. Erick disappeared during the night, around the same time the police turned up. He said later he was paranoid about getting caught with the Ecstasy!

I never really saw much of Erick after this, we did do another rave back in Shetland a few months later, it was on an island in a house. Everyone had to get to it in a rowing boat! We didn't make much money but it was fun doing. We then both started to do our own things, I started to traffic gear from Amsterdam and rumour has it Erick went on to sell drugs mail order and is now a lawyer!

Chapter 6 - Sam

December 1989 winter. I was in Greenwich one Friday in the Coach and Horses pub by the inside market with Jay. He said his girlfriend's niece Sam was coming to visit tomorrow and was I interested in meeting her. Jay had never met her but he said she was a year younger than me and about my height and pretty good looking by all accounts, I said "yes". I'd had a few girlfriends before but nothing really lasted, guess I was too involved in selling drugs. Maybe that's just what I needed a serious relationship, I was excited.

Saturday night came and I put on my best T-shirt and jeans and left for Greenwich. I was to pick Sam up from Linda's, Jay's girlfriend's flat. Julian and Linda would be waiting for us in the Rose and Crown pub just up the road.

I knocked at the door, there was a loud humming noise coming from the other side, I knocked again. The door opened and what I can only describe as a woman answered, what I mean by woman is not a girl. She looked amazing, mature and dressed in a red top with a short black skirt with red lipstick on her lips. Definitely not looking 18 years old and more like 25. "You must be Aaron, come in I'm just doing some hovering" she said, I went in.

Well that was it, I was in Love the first time I saw her face, we spent that Christmas together. Sam rented a room in Charlton from a friend of Linda's, his name was Chevy (he looked like Chevy

Aaron

Chase) and I sort of moved in with her, I used to stay there most nights. Christmas was a magical one; it snowed right through until February. We used to hit all the local bars, restaurants and clubs with Linda and Jay, a special favorite of mine was Jewels Holland's place 'Up The Creek' and a wine bar called 'Cobwebs' on the Greenwich one way system. Times were good I had a beautiful girlfriend, a nice car and quite a bit of money coming in from dealing Cannabis. I had no worries in the world and enjoyed every moment of it. All four of us were living it up and we got into doing drugs especially cocaine over the period. This was the first time I had actually bought drugs for my own consumption, a practice which would plague me for portions of the rest of my life.

Me and Sam when we first met 1989

Aaron Phyall

Jay and Lynda

Aaron

Chapter 7-*Extract from chapter 19* (St Martin's)

Canterbury, Kent winter 2005: I felt the Ambulance slow down and drive over speed bumps, my heart was pounding; we had arrived at St. Martins Mental facility "You're okay" the paramedics kept saying, they were trying to reassure me, they could see I was distressed. The ambulance doors opened and two large male nurses appeared both dressed in white tops. They asked me to leave the ambulance. I left the Ambulance and followed one of them, the other one walked behind me. At the entrance to the ward there were two double doors, one of the nurses spoke into an intercom on the wall and the doors opened, we walked in. Opposite us there were another two double doors, as the doors behind us closed the doors in front opened, a bit like an airlock.

I remember as I walked inside the main building there was a door on the left, it was open and I could see inside, there was a room. The walls of this room were all padded in a white cushiony fabric. I guessed it was a padded cell, just like you see in the movies. I was shitting myself and prayed it wasn't where they were going to put me. We carried on past the room to my relief and to a seating area in the distance, "You can sit here and wait... you're okay" the nurses kept saying. I sat down and waited and the nurses left.

Chapter 8 - Amsterdam

Charlton, London Spring 1990: The late nights and cocaine was taking its toll, I was getting into work later and later each week. I was still working for Masonry Services but out on site at Canary Wharf, and on my own. I hardly see the bosses so they were not aware I was starting work at 11am every day. As time went on my enthusiasm for the job just got worse, the work was mundane and I found myself thinking about Egypt, Tutankhamun and the pyramids at the Giza Plateau. I decided to leave my job and go there.

That evening I asked Sam to come with me, she had just started a new job in the city but still said yes, I think she really liked me, could this be the women I finally marry I wondered. The next few weeks were a mad rush to get everything ready, our passports, vaccinations and air tickets. We decided to backpack and bought a Lonely Planet's Guide book to help us find our way. It was so exciting getting things ready we were both really looking forward to the trip. This was to be the second time Sam had been abroad with me. I had been to Canada, France, and spent a lot of time in the Netherlands, especially Amsterdam.

I had been spending a lot of money lately and what was needed was a quick influx of cash to make sure we would have enough money for a long trip abroad. I decided Sam and I should go on a trafficking mission to Amsterdam. The plan was to get the ferry to Calais and drive through

Aaron

Belgium and into the Netherlands, reaching Amsterdam the next morning. I would arrange delivery of the gear from a Dutch guy I've done business with in the previous year. We would then do a bit of site seeing and then drive back.

Late one evening we arrived at Dover and took the ferry over to France. We disembarked and headed for the Belgium boarder. The boarder into and out of Belgium was now nonexistent and the one in and out of the Netherlands was still there but you didn't get stopped very often, not like the year previous when they were stopping everyone. I got stopped with four kilos of Morocco's finest stashed in the car but got away with it! Just about.

Most of the journey was motorway apart from the little bit from France to Belgium. We had only one music tape in the car, it was 'Bat Out Of Hell' by Meatloaf, Sam put it on. It took us about 6 hours to reach Amsterdam and we must have listened to the tape 10 times, I can still remember most of the words! Morning came and we approached the city. I was feeling very tired, Sam had been sleeping. We headed through the small winding streets in the car, I was being careful not to hit any of the trams; they seem to come out of nowhere sometimes. I parked the car near to Central Station in a back street and we both made for the Central Coffee Shop just across the road. This was where we would meet the Dutch guy, he was the owner.

In Amsterdam at the time coffee shops were only

tolerated selling Cannabis by the police. It's the same now but only for the customer's personal use. We had to be careful you could still get nicked if you were buying a shit load. I had decided to take back only about ¾ of a kilo, but of premium gear and not the commercial soap shaped bars I normally got. This was because I had found there was a market for something different back home and also it would reduce the sentence if we got caught on the way back.

We entered the café and the Dutch guy was sitting behind the bar, he looked pleased to see me. I'm not surprised as I think back, I'm sure he was charging me top money for the gear I bought from him. He was probably thinking Christmas is here again. It was first thing in the morning so the place was empty, we sat down and the Dutch guy brought us both over a large a cup of coffee and joined us. I discussed what I wanted 500 grams of soft Nepalese and 250 grams of Indian Cashmere. Cashmere is a water-based gear and quite mild but the effects last a long time, I had smoked it a couple of times before. The Dutch guy said he could sort it and to come back in the afternoon, I said okay then Sam and I left.

I spent the next few hours giving Sam a brief tour of the city, the mime artists at the square at the railway station, the red light district and the cannabis and sex museums. I knew she was nervous about the trip but I think she enjoyed the tour.

Aaron

We returned to the Coffee shop and the Dutch guy signalled to me as the place was full of people, he had sorted it. I left Sam in the shop and followed him through the back of the place and then up the stairs. We were in his office, I had been there before. He pulled a bag from under the table and placed it on the desk, I could smell the gear although it was still in the bag, it smelt strong. I took the bag and took out the stash, it was pucker and in 3 x ¼ kilo pieces. I handed it back to him and said "can you wrap it for me", he said "sure".

First he took some rubber gloves and put them on, then took some cling film and wrapped up the three blocks into three parcels. He then reached down into his drawer and pulled out a tub of talcum powder and shook it over the table. Once this was done the parcels were rolled around on the table and another wrapping of cling film was placed around them; this was done to take away any scent so the drug dogs couldn't smell it. Finally, brown box tape was wrapped around each parcel; you could see he had done this many times before. I remember paying the equivalent of £1700 for the 750 grams in Guilders; there were no Euros then! This was a lot of money for ¾ of a kilo, I used to pay about £900 for 1 kilo of the Moroccan soaps, but this Nepalese and Cashmere was top gear I could sell it for £180+ an ounce and it would be gone in a week. I left the Dutch guy counting his money in the office, went down the stairs and left the shop with Sam.

We made for the car and it had gone! Sam was

going mad, "how can someone nick the car" she was shouting, I was pissed off too, how were we going to get home? I stopped a police man on his bike and explained what had happened. He said it had been towed away as it was in a no parking spot; I had failed to notice this. I had to spend the last of our money to get it out of the pound! I just had enough left to get petrol to get back to the UK.

We arrived at Dover Customs and were both very nervous, we drove through and an officer waved us over, my heart stopped! "Please get out of the vehicle" he said. A whole team of customs officers then started taking the car apart; we just sat down on the curb and thought well that's it! The inside door trims were coming off and they were searching in the cushions, tapping the sills and bodywork and looking in the boot, they even x-rayed the spare wheel. After about an hour they let us go, I couldn't believe they didn't find the gear. I have never been so relieved in all my life; Sam was quite cool throughout the whole situation. We got onto the A2 and she asked me where I put it," I put it behind the radio and down the back of the dashboard lights! "I replied. We were so lucky!

Aaron

Chapter 9 - Egypt

Stansted Airport 3 weeks later. Mum and Dad had dropped us off; we made our way to the airline check in desk. We were flying with Tarom a Romanian airline via Bucharest, most flights to Egypt those days were via somewhere or another. We got our boarding passes and proceeded to security. Security back then was a bit of a joke it consisted of a few metal detector frames and a table with a couple of officers sitting on it drinking coffee. The idea was you walked through the metal detector, which never went off even if you were carrying metal objects. You then got frisked by a guy whatever the metal detector did and that was it! I cannot recall a bag scanner at Stansted at this time, although I remember seeing them at Toronto airport a few years earlier. There were never any long queues unlike today, it was bliss.

We boarded the aircraft and made our way to our seats, I could smell tobacco as we moved through the aircraft, everyone was smoking! I must say the plane was in a bit of a state; ripped and broken seats. My one, the back had moved right forward until it wedged behind the back of the seat in front, I could tell by the look on Sam's face this made her very nervous. I called the air hostess over, a large butch woman in her mid-forties, she also was smoking. She grabbed the top of my seat and flung it back, there was a loud crash, "are good" she said in a Romanian accent. She walked off, we sat down.

The flight to Bucharest was about 4 hours and not too bad from what I remember. The best part came for me when we reached the airport in Romania. We disembarked the aircraft to be greeted by soldiers on the tarmac, it was snowing. They were all lined up in camouflaged combat gear with rifles on their backs, they all looked very feminine. A closer look would reveal they were all women and most had bleached hair with full makeup on. Some of them were even wearing black high heels, Sam and I found this most amusing. We were directed from the ramp and off the plane to a large hanger type building, I remember it being very cold. Once inside the structure we had another security check and this time I enjoyed being frisked much to Sam's disapproval.

We had about 6 hours wait inside the hanger which was their terminal building. Birds were flying around the place pooing everywhere and there wasn't much to do. Finally we boarded the second leg of our flight to Cairo. I think we both got a chance to sleep for a while, all I remember of this flight is the approach to the airport as it was night and there weren't many lights on below us. Normally you see an abundance of patterns from street lights, cars and buildings when landing in a major city. Cairo at this time wasn't like this I only saw a few. We landed, went through customs and collected our rucksacks.

The next part of our journey was very stressful for both of us. We left the airport and it was like being

Aaron

beamed down to another planet. It was hot, very hot, there was a wave of skinny looking men all dressed up in what I know now as 'Galabyas' (traditional Egyptian clothing). They were all coming towards us," take your bag, take your bag" they kept saying, "Go away" I said," we have rucksacks" they didn't understand. They all swarmed around us "where you from" they shouted. Sam was distressed and so was I. We pushed through them and made for the money changing kiosk, which our guidebook said was near the exit of the airport. After a lot of panic we found the kiosk and changed up some money. We then jumped into a cab and made for the pre-planned hotel we had decided on. Heaven knows how we explained to the cab driver where to go but we managed it, the driver didn't speak English and this only added to the stress of everything.

We got to the hotel and it was late, It was the pits and probably 150+ years old; not that I think old hotels are the pits, it was under maintained and had shared bathrooms. We had a small dingy room with brown stained walls and fan on the ceiling. This type of accommodation is something which I have now got used to seeing throughout my travels but it was a shock to both me and Sam at this time. I later learnt this was a nice place compared to what the Egyptian people were putting up with. I closed the door then Sam just went into a fit of tears, "I want to go home" she cried, so did I! Although I never said so. I comforted her and said, "We will wait and see what happens tomorrow". I then decided to go and get something for us both to eat. I left the hotel.

It was Ramadan, although I had no idea what this actually meant, I still don't. I was aware that it could be bad for us though because it was difficult to get hold of alcohol. Something Sam and I used to indulge in frequently. I was walking down the street and saw what I thought was a small white baby cow or it could have been a skinny sheep. There were loads of people gathered around it, it looked like they were about to kill it there and then for food, something which disgusted me at the time; this was years before I realised what we do to chickens and our farm animal. At this point a saw a sign for a Kentucky fried chicken shop just down the street, I thought this was strange and didn't realise the Kernel had ventured out this far! I decided something from home may cheer Sam up so I followed the sign and bought a bargain bucket and went back to the room. She did like it; we ate the lot and then slept.

We awoke the next day to the sound of what can only be described as a man crying. I looked out the window and saw a speaker bolted to the wall, the sound was coming from this. How bizarre I thought, we later found out this was a regular occurrence every morning and in the afternoon and evening across the entire country. It was something to do with Ramadan we presumed. I decided I should read the guidebook we had brought with us; I did hate reading though and put it off until another day.

Aaron

We left the hotel and hit the streets; I remember how chaotic everything seemed, cars puffing deep black smoke into the air, donkeys pulling carts and people walking around in all direction, it was most disorientating. We just walked around in a confused state, well I know I did.

I cannot remember how long we were in Cairo and what we actually did entirely, but do remember the trip to the Cairo museum. We entered the museum grounds and the main building was in front of us, it was a lot smaller than I expected and had large carved granite statues at the entrance. I proceeded to try and impress Sam with my knowledge of granite Egyptian carvings but seemed to be boring her, so I proceeded into the main building. As we entered the entrance I could see it out of the corner of my eye, on the far right in a separate room. The burial mask of Tutankhamun was in the building! How please was I, I didn't expect to see it here. As soon as we paid and got through security I made a beeline for it with Sam in tow.

God it was impressive, all covered in gold with an aqua blue inlay of enamel, piercing eyes, with the glare of the Gods. It was about the same size as the copy I had done in Portland stone at college in London. It was in an old cabinet and I remember it didn't look that secure, looking back now if I'd known about Batman (called Batman because he couldn't go anywhere without robing) and his brother Ferret (Ferret because he looked like a ferret) I'd sometimes wonder if they could have stole it for me. We looked around the rest of the museum for a while and then made our way back to the hotel.

Around the next day we decided to visit the Pyramids at Giza. Giza is a plateau just west of the city and a borough of Cairo. I remember we got a taxi there or maybe a lift from someone. As we headed south I could see something solid start to appear in the distance, the city's pollution and sand which was caught in the air started to clear. It was the pyramids, first the largest one then the other smaller ones. The plateau or the area of the pyramids was sparse, there weren't that many buildings and the ones there were, were dwarfed by the main pyramid, it's massive! And so was the sphinx.

The Sphinx and Pyramids at the Giza Plato, Cairo Egypt

Aaron

I remember being heckled by hawkers into various tourist shops, which sold carpets, perfume and wonderful shaped bottles. I think we both felt a little safer here as most people had a good understanding of English. We visited a camel market where I was offered six camels for Sam from a trader; she quickly asked how much for me, he replied six chickens!

We took our first camel ride around the plateau, mine was called Mickey Mouse and Sam's was called Donald Duck; I'm not sure what the owner who named them was thinking! These beasts really make some strange noises and they dribble like made and don't mention the smell, they stunk! After this we made the short walk over to the main pyramid and past the Sphinx. I had remembered reading somewhere that someone thought the head of the Sphinx had been re-carved from a lions as the pharaohs head was a lot smaller than the body. I went and took a closer look, you could see where the mane of the lion might have run, if it had everything would have looked in proportion, I agreed with whoever wrote that. We arrived at the main pyramid and I just stood there and gazed above at its beauty. It must have looked even more astonishing with its coping stones still in place; these have been stripped off over the years and gave it its true pyramid shape. Some are still left at the very top; they glistened in the desert sun. I remember thinking whilst standing there all this built for just one pharaoh. I had read the work force was massive and the foundations of the pyramids only differ by two inches each side, what an accomplishment by the people of the time! I was thinking we would find it difficult to replicate this now using all our fancy equipment. We made our way past the Sphinx to the main pyramid.

Me and Sam on Mickey Mouse and Donald Duck

As I remember, I think the entrance to the pyramid was a bit of a way up, then as you got inside it there was a steep drop through a small shaft with a hand rail each side. The shaft went right to near the bottom of the foundations of the place. As you reached the bottom there was a room or what is known as the burial chamber, this was quite small and could not fit many of us in there, it had very high ceilings. Above were large slabs of granite holding up the masonry, they must have built the pyramid around this room I remember thinking. Inside the room there was what I was told was a burial casket. I think it had a lid to it but cannot quite remember. Sam wanted to leave by now but I could have stayed there for ages, the temperature was so very cool and was a welcome escape from the heat back on the plateau. We left the room after about 20 minutes and made our climb out. When we got out I took some pictures of Sam standing on the blocks which made up the pyramid.

Years later I looked at these closely I just couldn't believe these blocks were made by hand, in my opinion they were made using some sort of machinery and so were the building of the blocks into the pyramids!

We left Cairo going north on a bus to check out the coast and county of Alexandra. Our stay here was not long we only wanted to see the beaches. Port Said as the name suggests is a major port, a true shipping town full of bustling markets selling souvenirs like marble carvings and all types of handicrafts, I'm sure whatever you wanted could be found here. The streets were filled with men smoking Shisha (a water pipe), something I never got to try although it did look interesting. We found a place to stay that night and left the hotel to have a walk around. I must say, although the town was very manic Sam and I both felt safe unlike in Cairo, there was a mystical feeling about the place. We went in and out of shops experiencing our first attempts at haggling. A lot of the shopkeepers thought Sam was Egyptian and at first tried to speak to us in their language. We met a tour guide who invited us to an Egyptian meal at a place on the sea front, it was lovely. I lent him our guidebook to have a look at, he lost it! Or so he said. I knew I should have read it properly I remember thinking. We had to spend the rest of our adventure blind as there was no way of replacing it.

We took the bus back to Cairo the next day and caught a train south towards Luxor. We decided to make for a town called Hurghada, which was on the coast of the Red Sea. Someone had suggested we make for this place as it would be an experience travelling on an Egyptian train, we could also get a boat from there to the coral reefs of what is now called the Red Sea Riviera.

Aaron

The train turned up at the station in Cairo, it looked quite impressive and a lot newer than I had expected. The only thing was there were people sitting on the top of it, not just a few but hundreds, we both found it very funny, "I hope you have booked 1st class Aaron, I'm not sitting up there" Sam said. I had booked first class and the inside of the coaches were immaculate, they all had air conditioning and large blue comfy seats. As we pulled away from the station people started jumping from bridges onto the top of the train, something that looked very dangerous. The journey took about 8 or 10 hours from what I can remember. It gave us both chance to have our first good sleep.

Arrival in Hurghada was much like arriving at the airport in Cairo. People wanting to carry your bags, hawkers and a lot of beggars. It took us a while to find somewhere to stay. We met up briefly with an English couple; it was nice to have some conversation and talks about back home. It seemed as if we had been away for ages, we were both missing our home comforts. Sometime the following evening the English guy and me decided to try and get some gear. We just asked people in the street for it, something which I realise now was a stupid thing to do, especially in an Arabic country. Anyway after a while we got lucky and a local man pointed us towards a corner of the street. There were a group of Egyptians standing around all dressed up in local attire and I approached them. One of them pulled out a block of a brown substance which looked like an ounce. I took it from him and burnt the corner with my lighter expecting a nice pungent cannabis smell to fill the air, instead there was a horrible synthetic aroma, it was henna! A substance used by the Moroccans to cut their dope. When heated it's meant to be used to wash and dye hair. I promptly gave it back to the man and we made a quick retreat. He wasn't impressed at our discovery of his scam. This was the only time I tried to get drugs in Egypt... thankfully.

The next day we said our goodbyes to our new English friends and made our way to the boat. The boat was very small it could hold only about 20 of us and I remember thinking the crossing wouldn't take that long, how wrong was I, it lasted all day! I didn't realise small boats like this could travel so far, the crossing was bad it seemed to go on forever. Sam was really sick for most of it, she had to keep running to the stern to throw up. Finally we reached Sharm el Sheikh which is on the peninsular of the Sinai desert bang in the middle of the Red Sea. We were both relieved to reach dry land.

We took a coach to Dahab a place about 2-3 hours up the coast. To tell you the truth there wasn't much there apart from sand and a few dwellings. The beach was a different matter though, stretched along it for a couple of miles were about 10 compounds with beach huts and rooms inside. The compounds all had hippie names like Rainbow Lodge and Mr Smiley's

Aaron

Place. We spent a few hours looking around them all and eventually found a suitable one to stay in.

The place we chose was on the beach front and the enclosure had small round huts with straw roofs. Inside the huts were mattresses to sleep on, it wasn't very modern but all painted white and very clean. There were also hot showers. We spent the rest of our time in Egypt at this place it was very relaxing.

Sam one night at the huts in Dahab

Me in the Sinai desert

Sam was quite happy sunning herself on the beach; I on the other hand wanted to do something more exciting and decided to try out scuba diving for the first time. I booked a half days introductory course with the dive school next door. It was one of the most tranquil times of my life. I had a brief theory lesson in the class room which lasted an hour or so, then I got kitted up in the scuba gear and it was off to the beach for the experience. I was the only student.

Me and the instructor walked into the sea, Sam was watching. I bent my legs and the water was just below my shoulders. I put my regulator in my mouth and sunk my head below the water line. Oh my god, now this was definitely like being on another planet, I was thinking. There were fish everywhere, blue, red, pink, yellow in fact every colour you can think of, they were swimming around in swarms to a back drop of a vibrant coral reef which was bursting with life; I was truly mesmerized. The undersea world of Egypt looked so organised and clean; everything seemed to have a place and knew exactly what it was doing. Things looked automatic and structured and so different from the chaotic Egypt above me. The instructor appeared in front of me and signed to ask if I was okay, I replied with the appropriate sign back, I was more than okay, I was in Heaven. My first dive lasted only 20 minutes and it was something I will never forget, I didn't get to dive again until Australia 10 years later.

I did a lot of thinking when I was in Dahab, it was the longest time I had spent away from home, I was not running around trafficking and selling Cannabis or getting into other illegal situations, I had time to relax. I was off coke and thinking on a straight level, I started to realise how wrong I had been to sell drugs and decided to give it up. We both decided to get jobs and buy a house on our return.

Stansted Airport 6 weeks after we left: Mum and Dad picked us up, I remember being pleased to see them, they were pleased to see us. Sam had given up her room at Chevy's so my parents said she could stay with us in Gravesend for a while. She moved into my small box room, it was a bit of a squeeze.

We both spent the next few weeks looking for local jobs, I found one first with a firm called Medway Memorials in Rochester. I was to be making headstones for dead people, something which I wasn't looking forward to at the time. Sam managed to get a job in the local town working for Anglian Windows as a receptionist a few weeks later. I then give Burma (my brother) all my drug dealing contacts as I decided I was now 20 years old and going straight, I'd try and live a normal life with Sam.

We both had jobs but the money we were earning was nothing like I was used to, Sam was getting about £400 a month, I got paid weekly and after tax and was only earning around £150. My float was diminishing, Egypt and the cocaine abuse and high end living before we left the country had taken a large portion of it. We started to save like mad for a deposit on a house.

About four month later we had saved enough, it was coming to the end of the summer and we were both eager to find a place to live. We decided to look around the Medway town's area as it was a lot cheaper than Gravesend and closer to my works. We found a small place on the far side of Chatham, it consisted of two bedrooms, a neat small garden, kitchen, bathroom and had a downstairs cloakroom, it was only about 4 years old and a repossession. We put in an offer of £46,000, it was accepted. We were both ecstatic.

Aaron

Chapter 10-*Extract from chapter 19*(St Martins)

Canterbury, Kent winter 2005, I was sitting in the seated area down the corridor from the entrance of the mental facility on my own, a nurse approached me. She said we need to check you over and proceeded to take my blood pressure, I let her. Then another one approached with a large trolley with drawers and said she needed some blood. I thought about this and said no! I have a phobia towards needles you see. Also I have a theory that this only gives someone in a lab something to do and creates jobs within the NHS, the doctors thought I was being paranoid. I had a complete blood works done at a private hospital in Bangkok 18 month previously, when a few strange experiences led me to have a full medical. This never revealed anything wrong with me, apart from a low white blood cell count which I knew about and have had since I was a kid. The nurse walked off. The other nurse proceeded to take my blood pressure and said it was very high, I said, "well what do you expect, I've just been sectioned and bundled into an ambulance by the police!" She smiled and walked off. I didn't think it was very funny although she had a great smile; I was fuming about what had happened to me that evening but scared and shaking like a leaf inside.

The next thing I knew was my parents and brother walking down the corridor towards me, this made me even more annoyed for they were the ones which had instigated me being sectioned that night. I cannot remember what exactly happened next there and then but we had a big argument about how I had been treated by them the past few days. I thought they were out of order especially after I had only just been released from my first admission from a psychiatric ward. My brother was saying something about me saying to him previously we could all be living in a computer and this is why he thought I was mad. This is something which I had said, although I didn't totally agree with within myself, there was an element in my mind at this time which wondered if it could at all be possible. "So what are we all living in then? " I commented to him, there was no answer. Because of the shouting and disruption to the ward the nurses asked them to leave.

A nurse showed me to my room. The rooms at St. Martins were quite nice, large and spacious. This was the first time I had ever been here as my 1st admission was to Elmstone ward in Margate. The nurse offered me a sleeping tablet with a glass of water, I couldn't convince myself to take it, for various reasons I will not go into now, I said no. The nurse left and I proceeded to put my things away and get undressed. By now I was beginning to calm down and getting used to the fact I was going to be spending 28 days here, under a section 2. This was the amount of time given to the doctors to make an assessment of me but if they wanted to keep me after the 28 days they could put me on a section 3 which is for 6 months. Then after this it's a year's contract and you never get out! I had one last chance before I got caught up in this spiralling cobweb of hospital incarceration. At the moment they could only hold me for 24 hours so I had to convince a doctor and social worker in the morning I was in a fit mental state, if not I would be on a section 2 and thought all would be lost. I slept.

Chapter 11 - Moving from House to House

Chatham, Kent 1991. We had been in our house for about a year and things were going great. I had gone self employed and was still working for Medway Memorials but as a sub contractor. My money had increased and we decided to move house. I had not returned to my old ways of the end of the late 80's and was still on the straight and narrow. We had both spent the past year doing up the house, just painting and landscaping the garden. It really gave us a feel for DIY so we decided to get an old place and do it up.

Eventually we found somewhere and it was in my home town of Gravesend. It was an old place 1930's style semi with bay windows, three bedrooms and a massive garden. The only thing was it needed everything doing to it, new bathroom and kitchen, windows and conservatory, central heating and re-wiring. The garden needed landscaping too. We moved in just before winter and eagerly set about restoring it.

Aaron

Our second house at Gravesend, Kent, UK

September Sam had bought me a book by Paul McKenna on hypnosis it was called 'The Hypnotic World of Paul McKenna'. I had been watching him a lot on TV with his stage hypnosis show and he was becoming quite a celebrity. I scanned through his book that winter, like I tended to do with all books and read the sections on how to hypnotise, at that time that is all I was interested in.

A few years later I read it properly and on reflection it helped me to figure out what was actually happening to my mind and I would start to begin to understand our blind views of the workings of this world we live in.

A guy from work Steven Ives, was going to a stage hypnosis evening at a working mans club in London. I asked him to get me a couple of tickets, he agreed. I had a Renault 5 GT turbo at the time and remember caning it though the Blackwell tunnel at 100mph on the way to the club, Sam was screaming. We arrived at the club and Ives met us in the reception. We went into the hall and he introduced us to some of his mates. An hour or so later the hypnotist arrived and yes he did have a medallion on! He immediately ask for volunteers, Sam and I both put our hands up much to the laughter of Ives and his mates. We walked out onto the floor and was asked to all stand in a straight line, music was then put on. He asked us all to count backwards from 100 in our heads. Then kept telling us to relax in a reassuring smooth accent and to move our heads down and up etc... After about 10 minutes of this he started to walk around to us all and whisper things in our ears, I burst out laughing and got sent back to the bar, but Sam and about 8 others were left standing there with their heads down. Well the next thing was he put on a Madonna track, Sam started to dance, she thought she was Madonna. He then took a chair and placed it in front of her; she started to dance around it. He then said something in her ear and she started to take her clothes off. Ives and his mates started cheering; I immediately rushed onto the floor and grabbed her! She was a little confused and didn't remember all of what she had been doing. We watched the rest of the show and then left. I tried to get Sam to let me try and hypnotise her back home after this, as it had described in the book she bought me but she wasn't having any of it! I think this experience scared her.

Aaron

This was the first time I begun to think about how much I didn't know about the mind and how other people could influence it easily.

Over the next 18 months we worked hard on the house. We used to get in from work and paint, re-wire and attempt to get it into to shape. We got a couple of ducks and a rabbit called Buffy, we were trying to build a bit of a home. It was getting too much for us though, most of our free time and money was spent on the house, new kitchen, new windows, new electrics the list went on. We both started to drink a lot over the weekends, especially me. The house had the potential to be a great place but we weren't happy. Sam lost her job and we decided to sell the house and move yet again.

We were driving in the country one day and we ended up in Ashford, quite a small place then and famous for it live animal stock markets. We see a sign for Bovis Homes the housing development company and decided to go and have a look. They were building new homes on farmland that had just been declassified as green belt, the setting was great and in a little cul-de-sac by a woods. It looked as if they were going to be building about 200-300 new houses on the site with other developers involved. We went into the show room to have a look and were advised of a couple of properties which were up for sale and within our price range. There were two detached houses for sale at that time and both had four bedrooms; one had all white rendering and the other a brick finish.

I chose the white one as I do like white, Sam got to pick the carpets, I had to put up with a pink carpet! We managed to do a part exchange with the old place in Gravesend, things moved very quickly and we had moved in by the spring 1994.

We had our ideal house and things were going great, over the next year Sam got a new local job working for Coty Rimmel (the Makeup Company) and I continued working In Rochester at Medway Memorials. Things were going great again.

The internet was just taking off over here and everyone was all excited about this new technology. I decided to build a new computer. I had been into computers before as a kid and was a bit of a wiz when it came to them. One day when reading peoples home pages; which was what the net mainly consisted of back then. I found some guys in India that were advertising granite memorials for manufacture, I decided to send them a fax. I got a reply with their company information and prices and couldn't believe how cheap they were. They could offer me a basic black granite memorial and base for £30 ex shipping, as I understood it my boss at Medway was paying about £180 for the same thing in this country and he had some good contacts. The mark up retail was massive about £600.

I ordered some samples to be sent by air freight at first, just so I could see the quality of their work. The samples consisted of about 5 or 6 memorial granite bowl turned vases, all polished, they were

Aaron

well made and of excellent quality granite. I paid about £8 for them each and the air transit was about £400 in total. They still sold for about £200+ each, the money to be made was better than in cannabis and completely legal. I decided to go to India and meet them.

Chapter 12 – India

Bangalore, India April 1995: I had decided to bring my brother Burma to India with me; he was good with money and had a good business sense. We arrived at Bangalore airport on a Jet airways flight from Bombay (Mumbai). On our exit from the airport Claudius met us. Claudius is a cousin of an aunt of mine who had written to him saying we were going to be in India and would he make sure we were okay. Claudius had said yes and made us feel at home from the start. He insisted that we stay with him and his family for a few days and wouldn't let us stay in a hotel. We both welcomed his hospitality.

He had a small van and I got in the front and Burma jumped in the back with the bags. As soon as we left the airport the traffic began, it was dark and a hot night with bumper to bumper traffic. Every car driver was hooting their horn; the piercing sound was going through my head. Burma was laughing and saying maybe they were trying to play a tune.

Claudius showed us all the in places to eat and drink and dance in the city, NASA club was a favourite place of mine. It was quite small and covered in chrome and there were red lasers shining everywhere. We went to bars that wouldn't have looked out of place back home. We couldn't believe what we were seeing; this was not the India we had expected. It turns out that later we discovered Claudius was showing us the upper

Aaron

class side of the city where the rich hang out. Although India was up and coming I would later discover on future trips some of the poverty that lay under a façade of extravagance and a cast culture. We stayed with Claudius and his family for a few days, he then organised the train journey for us down south to Coimbatore, this was where the granite suppliers were.

Me and Burma in a Pub in Bangalore, India

My brother and Claudius, Bangalore 1995

It was a night train we took, and colonial in style. It looked very old and nothing like the one Sam and I had taken in Egypt 5 years earlier. This was the first time we had chance to speak with the average Indian person. I was impressed at their English and in many respects it was better than mine and Burmas as they sounded like ex private school pupils, where as we had common Gravesend accents. Claudius had arranged for a guy to stay outside our cabin to make sure no one bothered us. It made me feel very important. This is something I felt on the whole of my first trip to India because the average Indian person was hospitable and well mannered towards us, unlike the upper classes who were horrible, self centred and arrogant. We reached our destination in the morning and were met by Mr Elangoven at the train station; he was the guy that had made the turned bowl vases at his factory. I later named him Mr E as I could not pronounce his full name.

He took us to his factory to have a look around, it was quite big and he employed about 15 people. His main business was exporting to Australia. The three of us then took a ride on an auto rickshaw to meet his mate who was in the granite business too. The ride was something which we all enjoyed, it was great. The rickshaw had three wheels one at the front and two at the back, it had a four stroke engine. The three of us sat in the back and we took a trip around the village at speed. Finally we reached Mr Tangelveail factory and I named him Mr T, his place was a lot bigger than Mr E's and he had some large saws and flat bed polishers. After a quick tour around the factory we went to his office. Once there we discussed prices for them both making the Bowl vases and Headstones. I couldn't believe how inexpensive they were. Burma and I then decided we could sell four 20 ton containers full of memorials per year starting 12 months from then, as soon as we worked out the prices we got over excited on how much money we could make. We then took a trip to their bankers to seal the deal. We signed paper work confirming this so Mr E and Mr T could arrange finance for the shipments. We weren't that bothered about signing as we had no formal company anyway so it didn't matter if we defaulted. They then took us on a tour of the surrounding area over the next few days, quarries, factories and a hill station. They were most hospitable.

The Guys from Mr E's workshop

Me and Mr.E at a Hill Station in Coimbatore India

Mr T's workshop

Aaron

Before our trip home we decided to jump on a plane to Goa and check out the beaches, Anjona market and the scene. When we got there we were both tired from all the travelling and just wanted to recuperate. We found a place to stay and rented a motor bike and visited some of the local sites and beach bars. We stayed in Goa for about a week; there wasn't much happening it was out of season, we then made our way back home to the UK.

After returning to the UK I had to try and raise the money for the first container. I tried the bank but was already maxed out on my mortgage. I did manage to get enough cash for a part load (about 2 ton) which was shipped in a container with a load of textiles; I had to go to Felixstowe to pick it up in a van. I sold the lot over a period of 4 months but I would have to get involved with one of my old drug contacts to help finance a whole shipment!

Chapter 13 - The Wedding

Ashford UK Spring 1996: Everyone seemed to be getting married at that time, me and Sam thought as we had been living with each other for a while, we should as well. I never actually asked her, I just kind of fell into it. We planned it for the summer, only 5 months away. I was still trying to raise the cash for the container of memorials and wondered how we were going to afford them both. Anyway, I put the container out of my mind and blagged India to hold on for a while until I could get the finance sorted.

The day of the wedding arrived, I had been staying with Burma and my mates in a hotel just up the road for the night, we had been doing loads of cocaine. Burma had got 14 grams of the proper stuff from Jason; Terinse's brother my supplier from the Shetland days. We were all up all night and got totally out of it. Morning came and we looked worse for ware, especially me. Burma was my best man and Karl and James; friends from my school days were ushers. We made for the church. Everyone was already there, about 80 family and friends turned up for our big day. I did my best and stood outside the place attempting to talk to everyone for a while, I was still hung over.

My brother signalled for me to go into the Church as he saw Sam arriving down the road. At this point I seemed to go into automatic mode and I cannot remember much of the service. I do remember looking around and seeing Sam and

Aaron

her dad walking down the aisle. Although I did want to marry her I remember thinking I didn't want to be there and felt self conscious and out of place. The rest of the service went fine apart from an attack of giggles by Sam. It was then outside for some photographs and off to the reception.

I began to relax a bit here especially after a trip to the toilets for a line or two. Then it was a few short speeches and a buffet meal. The evening arrived quickly, the DJ set up and we had a dance. Then Jason turned up with some more sniff, I must say at various points in the day I didn't have a clue what was going on, I was out of it!

Me and Sam

Aaron

I hadn't seen Jason for about five years and he was bragging about how well he and his brother Terinse were doing in the drug scene. He said that they had made quite a bit of money and was looking for something legit to get involved in. I immediately said about the containers of memorials I had on order from India and asked him if they wanted to get involved. I explained I needed £20,000 to pay for the shipments, he agreed to lend it to me. I was pleased but also a bit apprehensive as I had wanted to put all that drug stuff behind me, but I needed the money. The rest of the wedding went okay we didn't have a honeymoon but planned to the following year. We stayed in a hotel that evening and returned to the house the next day.

A few months later Jason called and said he had got the money together and would I meet him in London to pick it up. I was relieved to hear I had finally managed to get someone to lend me the cash. I jumped in the car and proceeded up town. Jason was renting a house just on the outskirts of the city; I eventually found it and parked the car. I remember feeling nervous and apprehensive, I knocked at the door and Jason answered, "Come in mate" he said. I went in and we walked into the lounge. I noticed the place was in quite a mess, empty drink cans and takeaway cartons thrown across the place, something I wasn't expecting from someone about to give me 20 grand, the place looked like a squat. Jason disappeared out of the room and come back with a carrier bag full of cash, he said we better count it and we both proceeded to go through the wad. I remember thinking of the counterfeit days back when I was living with my mum. I wondered if it was real and asked Jason, he said, "Yes, I don't get counterfeit". I looked at some of it myself and it looked real enough. We had a brief conversation about the old days and I then left.

10 years ago £20,000 pound in cash was a lot of money to be carrying about, it still is. I made my way back to Ashford taking care not to speed or draw attention to myself. I spent the next few months slowly putting into my bank account in drips and drabs as I couldn't really account for where I got it all if asked by the bank. I then contacted India and confirmed a container.

It wasn't until about 10 months later that the container arrived as Mr T and Mr E had some manufacturing and despatching problems. The container arrived around September 1997. I had rented a small unit at a friend's yard in Longfield, Kent to store the memorials. We unloaded them all and checked that they were of good quality and workmanship, they were.

I set about selling it. I had given up my job at Medway Memorials much to the dismay of Sam and was planning to stay focused on making a go of this business. Everything went great at first, the memorial firms were buying it and I was saving enough money to pay Jason back. Then for some reason the trade stopped purchasing from me. Bill my old boss said it was because they didn't want anyone else in the industry. I think they were just jealous of me and annoyed that they didn't think of importing granite themselves, what ever the reason I was in trouble, I had only sold a quarter of the shipment and had to pay my mortgage and bills, the rent on the unit and what made things worse was Sam and I weren't getting on.

By Christmas Sam had left me and I went into a spiral of drink and drug abuse which lasted for the best part of three years. I had managed to let out the house in Ashford and move back in with my parents. I worked back at Medway Memorials for a while but couldn't keep it together. In the end I decided to sell the house the summer of 2000 and then hit the road.

The house sold for £175,000 and after I had paid off my debts was left with 60 grand. I paid Jason about £5,000, leaving the rest to pay later but on reflection wished I had paid him off in full.

Chapter 14 - Hitting the Road

Gravesend, Kent Winter 2000: My solicitor had just phoned me to say he had completed on the sale of the house and had deposited the proceeds into my brother's account as I instructed. I had asked him to do this because Sam had gone into bankruptcy a few years earlier. I had been getting letters from her creditors asking me for payment of her debts and thought it would be wise to pretend I had no money just in case. I went to the Halifax that morning and withdrew £2,000. I had decided to travel and leave the country. I spent the rest of that day packing my things and wondering where to go. In the end I decided to make for America, Florida in particular. I had developed a keen interest in flying over the past few years and had a few lessons. I would go to Florida and learn to fly a plane!

That evening I turned up at Gatwick airport with no ticket and £2,000 in my pocket. I couldn't get a flight to Florida, so decided to go to Toronto instead as I had family there and my Nan was visiting them at the time. As I got on the plane a big relief come over me, I was leaving all the stress from the divorce, the selling of the house and failure of my business behind me. Also the drink and cocaine I had been consuming over the past few years. In a way I was trying to leave all my past behind me and move to the future. I didn't realise it at the time but I would be away for nearly four years. Toronto, Florida, the Caribbean, Mexico and Vancouver the list went on. It wasn't a

Aaron

holiday it was more of a search, a search for a new beginning.

I arrived in Sydney one day and then flew on to Brisbane. I decided to make my way up the coast, Byron Bay, Early Beach, Frazer Island was some of the many places I visited. I had heard of a town called Anakie on my travels up the coast, it's famous for gemstones, Sapphires in particular. Someone said you could buy them quite cheaply there; I thought about this and wondered if this could be something I could get involved in. I met up with a mate from Gravesend (Gigs) who was already in Queensland travelling about and convinced him to join me.

Me at Frazer Island, Queensland, Australia 2002

We hired a vehicle and made for Anakie. On our arrival we found a pub which had rooms for rent, we decided to stay for a few nights. That evening we went into the pub for a drink. There was a couple of guys chatting in the corner, one of them had a wrap of paper in his hands and was showing it to the other guy. I thought they were selling drugs and I decided to approach them but when I got near I noticed it wasn't drugs but in fact gemstones. They asked me if I wanted to have a look and I said yes. As soon as they past me the wrap of paper I could see the stones twinkle in the light, a brilliant hue of yellow sparkled from them, something even now still mesmerises me. Anyway It turned out that these guys were gemstone prospectors and had just finished a shift at their Sapphire mine. We got chatting to them and in the end we were invited up to their claim to dig for gemstones the next morning.

We set off early about 5am and made our way in

Aaron

an old battered van towards the Australian bush where their mine was. When we got there it didn't look much, just a few pieces of machinery, shovels and picks. The mine was open cast which meant there were no tunnels to climb down, all you had to do was pick a small area and dig a small hole. The earth was then put in a bucket and poured into a rotating machine. The machine then graded the earth into different sizes; you could then look through it for Sapphires. We spent about 5 hours doing this; it was very tiring in the hot Australian sun. Then we both started to find small pieces of dark material, some green and some yellow. The guys we were with said it was Sapphire but of low quality and it was too dark and not worth cutting. Although this was the case I felt pleased I had found something, we then all retired to the pub for a few drinks. After this experience I read anything I could get my hands on to do with gemstones, to start with it would become a bit of a hobby of mine but later I would attempt to turn it into a career.

Aaron Phyall

Me at the Sapphire mine near Anakie, Queensland, Australia

I continued travelling around Australia for a while but couldn't find the new life and beginning I was looking for there. I had read in some of the books I had acquired on gemstones about Bangkok being the centre of the coloured gemstone industry and jewellery making business. In one of these books it mentions a guy called Ted Themelis, an American who was doing wonderful things with sapphires. He had managed to change their colour using heat and a chemical process, thus making worthless sapphires into sellable ones. He runs a course in Bangkok showing people how to do this and I decided to go there and enrolled on the course.

Aaron

Chapter 15 - Bangkok Nights

Bangkok September 2002: I arrived in Silom the main business street of the city. Ted had arranged for me to stay in a Hotel at the top of the street just up from the tourist part of Pat Pong. It was the evening and I was due to meet him the next day so I checked in the hotel then decided to go out and have a look around the city. There was a nice receptionist on the front deck called Lek, she really caught my eye, we would become more than just good friends. I asked her to call me a cab.

Pat Pong was a place I had heard of before; it's full of girly bars, restaurants and music venues. It also has a street market running down the centre. It consisted of two streets Pat Pong 1 and Pat Pong 2. I decided to make my way there.

I left the hotel and took the cab. Once inside the cab I instructed the driver to take me to Pat Pong, he said"you want woman" I said "No, just take me to Pat Pong". He then proceeded to show me pictures of naked women and say "very good women only 3,000 baht", I said "just take me to Pat Pong" in an aggressive manner. He then proceeded to do a u-turn and head down the street. He took me about 5 minutes down the road which wasn't that far; I could have walked it. He stopped by a load of taxis all jammed up at the side of the road, the police were trying to keep the traffic flowing past them. I got out the cab and was right in front of the market. Thai men were coming up to me and showing me pictures of women "you want women" they kept saying, they were right in my face and I pushed them away, they soon got the message. I then decided to check out the market.

Pat Pong market is large and you can buy any type of counterfeit goods you want: from shirts to watches, films and trainers, there was also a large selection of handy crafts. I spent a few hours looking around the place, it was interesting. Beside the market were strip joints and Go-Go bars which ran down the hole of the road. Go-Go bars were establishments full of women dressed in bikinis who danced on platforms and tables. Obviously they were all full of men gawking but with the odd women! In the next road was Pat Pong 2, this place had more bars and food stalls selling Thai dishes. It was when walking down here I noticed a sign saying English 'Fish and Chips', I hadn't had proper fish and chips for ages so I decided to follow it. The sign led me to an English themed pub called Bobby's Arms.

Aaron

Pat pong 1, Street market. Bangkok, Thailand

Inside there was a long rectangular bar all made of wood and behind the bar was a space for the staff to serve from. Sat around it were some gloomy face's who were mostly expatriates dressed in shirts and suits all reading copies of the Bangkok Post. I sat down and ordered a Carlsberg larger and was only sitting there for about five minutes reading the menu when I looked up to see a man with a big grin on his face looking at me. I said, "Hello" and we started chatting. It turns out his name was Jim and he was from the UK. He was a little chubby man and looked a bit like the late Benny Hill. He had been in Bangkok for years and knew the place like the back of his hand; we would go on to be good mates throughout my stay in Bangkok. He showed me about the place, the best bars to go to, what buses to take to get around the city and where to eat. I had a few beers and some fish and chips with him then I decided to make my way back to the hotel as I had to get up early in the morning.

The next day I awoke early, had to make my way down to the bottom of Silom to an adjoining Soi (Soi means side road in Thai) and decided to take the bus. There are three types of buses in Bangkok a blue one with air conditioning, another blue one with fans and a red one with no fans. As I was only going down the road I decided to take a red one. The journey was only 5 minutes and it cost 6 baht, not even 2 pence. I got off the bus and headed for Ted's place.

Ted lived in a typical Thai shop house, it was on three floors and he had his lab on the bottom floor. I had understood he was American but when I met him he had a Greek type accent, I'm not really sure where he came from. He greeted me at the door and welcomed me in to the lab. It was full of machinery, furnaces and large gas bottles. We walked through another room which he had made into a classroom. There were about five others sitting there at a table.

The course started and he went on about atoms, chemistry and a load of other stuff which was mostly way above my head. I remember thinking, just show me the process of changing worthless Sapphires into ones which were worth money, I don't really need to know all this atom shit. I

Aaron

guessed he had to hang it out to make us think we were getting value for money. Finally the practical stuff came and we made our way to the laboratory. He showed us some Corundum (the name for Ruby and Sapphire) from Burma, it was dark red in colour and just looked like a piece of dark rock, it wasn't translucent. He placed the material in a crucible with some beryllium and then into a furnace. It then had to be heated at least 1600 degrees for 6 hours, we left the lab and returned the next day. On the next day we all waited eagerly as the furnace was opened, there was a mess of light red deposits around the crucible, not what I had expected. I had expected to see glistening stones sparkling in the sunlight. When I approached Ted and said this to him, he said" well it has changed colour like I have said in my books". I was fuming I had come all this way and paid all this money to learn about something that would be of no use to me. I demanded my money back. Back then I was ignorant and didn't understand heat treatments and the way certain chemicals react with the atoms of a certain type, it could have been of use to me if only I had listened. I ended up storming out.

Well what was I going to do now I thought, so I phoned Jim. He said you have to be careful of expatriates in Bangkok as most of them are just after your money, a piece of advice I went by for the rest of my stay. I decided to stay in Bangkok for a while but I needed somewhere to live, the place where I was staying was okay but a bit expensive. Jim said there was a place just over the river called the 'World Residence' and that I should stay there. The next day I checked out the hotel and made my way across the river. I managed to get Lek's phone number, the receptionist on the front desk before I left.

The World Residence looked like a cheap doss house from the outside; it is located on a small one way street in the Klongsan district of the city. When you enter there is a large reception area bustling with activity. When I arrived I wasn't sure I wanted to stay there as it looked quite neglected and not usually the sort of place I would stay. Jim had said it was really nice so I thought I would check it out more. I went to the front desk and enquired about the price, they said in tower A its 8,000 baht per month (about £110) and tower B is 17,000 baht (£280) per month, I decided to look at tower B. The lady on reception took me through some doors into a car park, at this stage I thought it wasn't very nice but I would go and have a look anyway. Then we reached some stairs and once up the stairs we emerged into what I describe as an oasis of a building. The floors were covered in a light brown marble and the walls painted in white. There was a large swimming pool overlooked by balconies and a restaurant nestled in the corner. It looked great and had a Spanish feel to it all. I was surprised that this place was hidden behind an old run down building. This was to become my home for the next three months.

I really got to know the local area, the pubs and restaurants, even some of the local shop keepers.

Aaron

There was a place I was particularly fond of and that was the Thonburi café just off Ladya Road. It is a Thai Pub now but it used to be a theatre, when you walk in there is a small stage at the front with a sweeping staircase at the back leading to a large balcony. There is two of these theatres on top of one another, they wouldn't look out of place in London, the architecture looked very similar both inside and out, apart from the granite cladding and floors which looked as if it was done in the late 90's. The theatre downstairs was used for Thai karaoke and various games and was in a bit of a state. Upstairs was a different matter though, it may be in need of a bit of sprucing up but there were DJ's and Thai groups singing there every night, I really considered it to be somewhere special and developed a love for Thai music there. I could be found in there most nights listening to it.

A week or so past and I was getting a bit bored so I phoned up Lek; the secretary from the hotel I stayed in on Silom. She was pleased to hear from me and we arranged to go out one evening. Lek, which means small in Thai was very cute, she was about 27 but looked a lot younger as most Asians do; She was always happy and smiling. I think we probably went to the Thonburi Café on our first night out. I spent a lot of time with her in Bangkok and even got invited to a Thai wedding in her home town. Later on I end up staying with her and her two flat mates for a while.

Aaron Phyall

Lek in Ko Samui, Thailand 2002

I had decided I should get motivated as I had been partying with Lek and her friends for a while now and thought I should get back into the gem scene. I had heard of a Gemmology course that was being run by the Asian Institute of Gemmology Science (AIGS) on Silom. I went and enrolled on a 4 months crash course in gemstones. I would be learning how to grade stones, differ from synthetics and natural, and learn how they were formed.

It was the morning of my course and I needed to get to the city. The best way to Silom in the mornings from where I was staying was to take the bus from outside the hotel and then get a boat across the Chao Phraya River, then a motorcycle taxi to Silom. I tended to walk most days instead of getting a motorcycle as I considered them to be a bit dangerous in Bangkok. A cab ride from the

Aaron

hotel to Silom during the rush hour was out of the question, the roads just come to a standstill, a ride this way can take hours. My little route took about 45 minutes and was quite pleasant with the boat ride in between.

I arrived at the AIGS building. The school was situated in a tower about 40 floors up. You had to go through security at the main entrance as the building was also home to Gem businesses. I walked from the lift to the college doors and was greeted by a lady at the front desk, she showed me to the classroom. The class consisted of about 7 people; they were from different parts of the world and not Thai. One guy was from Russia, a woman from the Middle East and the rest from the USA, our teacher was also from the there.

I started to get into the course during the day and revising more in the evenings. I was finding it very demanding but was just about coping. Then one morning about I month into the course I began to feel unwell, my vision was blurred, I had been sick in the toilets and I was finding it hard to think. I thought I had caught a bug or something and had to go back to the hotel. I felt fine the next day but found it hard to get to sleep the previous night. I went to the college that day and the same thing happened but this time I was finding hard to write also. This went on for the next week or so and then I started to get slight hallucinations and distortions in my vision. I thought someone had spiked me with a drug! I was also feeling paranoid. I took a week off the course and felt a lot better.

I put me being sick down to a bug or may be stress, but looking back now I think this was the start of me possibly becoming unwell.

During my week off I decided to go down to the restaurant of the hotel to have a bite to eat. I noticed a guy sitting outside on a table; he was in his mid 50's and looked like Father Christmas without the beard. He was trying to do the crossword in the Bangkok Post. He started to mutter to himself something about, I've told that bloody Ralfi to do the crossword in pencil then rub it out afterwards. "Who's Ralfi" I said, "Oh he retired here years ago haven't you seen him about?" the bloke said. I said "no" we continued to chat for a while then the bloke introduced himself as John, and then left. I ordered a meal and proceeded to eat it, Just as I finished I heard a voice from behind me "have you seen John" it said. I looked up and saw a very skinny looking man in his late 60's, "Yes he just left" I replied. "Are you Ralfi" I said, "yes I am" he said, then he shuffled off into the distance. I would go on to meet these two characters on and off over the next week at the table outside the restaurant, we had some fascinating chats about Thailand.

Christmas was approaching and I had broken up from college, I had to go back there in the New Year to do six more weeks and then some final exams. I hadn't planned anything for Christmas but had been told by Jim who had since returned to the UK that they do a nice Christmas dinner at

Aaron

Bobbies Arms in Pat Pong. One morning I met up with John and Ralfi at the table outside the restaurant, I asked them if they would like to join me for Christmas dinner at Bobby's. John said yes but Ralfi wasn't that sure as he had an adopted Thai family he goes to eat with most days.

Christmas Day 2002 Bobby's Arms: We Walked along Soi 4 off Silom and entered the entrance to the pub. Bobby was at the front of the bar and handing out eggnog whilst wishing everyone a Merry Christmas. He was a big fat man quite short and from China, he spoke in a London English accent. I'm not that sure if he had ever been to London but he gave the impression that he had. The place was full of Schoolteachers and retired expatriates as it normally is, all eager to taste Bobby's cooking. There is one thing about Bobby and that is he knows how to cook western style. We had the best Christmas dinner ever; I would even go as far as saying it was as good as my Mums. John and I chatted about Bangkok and he told me how he had retired from working at Sotheby's in the UK two years earlier and how he had moved to Thailand to live. He was on the pull and hoping to eventually find a Thai woman.

It was New Years Eve 2003. I was in a restaurant on the banks of the Chao Phraya River. The fireworks were going off and lights could be seen from all above, it was a truly beautiful sight. To this day I have never seen fireworks like this; the Thai's really know what they are doing when it comes to explosives. There were explosions that formed into planets of blue, red and green, shooting stars that shot across the sky and rockets that exploded into the night from the bridges, a spectacular sight.

I was with John and Ralfi. We were sitting at the table eating our Phat-Thai when the conversation turned to gemstones as it nearly always does, me being a bit of a gemologist now. I cannot remember exactly how the conversation went as it was a long time ago but we were talking about gold and the state of the world. I said that money was backed up by gold, as most of us are taught in school, John said no its people. People I said how can money be backed up by people? He went on to say that if all the money in the world was divided up evenly then everyone would have a dollar a day to live on. At first I couldn't get my head around what he was saying but many years later I did.

In the New Year I joined the British club, a club mainly occupied by the British but there were a few Australians, Americans and Thais who were members. This place was a bit posh and set on a piece of land just off Silom. The main building was a glorious colonial styled structure with tennis courts, a swimming pool, restaurants and a bar. I started to spend most of my free time there and used it as a bit of an escape from the hectic surroundings of the city; a true oasis of a place. I used to take Lek there and her friend Mom, they really liked the swimming pool. I started back at college and things weren't going well, I was

Aaron

starting to lose my temper and just couldn't concentrate, I ended up having words with my teacher and walking out, I did the same thing as I did on Ted's heat treatment course, looking back a pattern was beginning to emerge.

I decided to leave the World Residence in the early part of March as it was getting expensive. I was running out of money, I had money back home but my family wouldn't send it to me as they thought I was spending it on drugs or just wasting it. I didn't have a place to stay and ended up wondering the streets one night, I decided to go and see Lek. She said I could stay with her and her roommate for a while if I liked, I was relieved and said yes.

The room Lek had was very small about 6x5 meters in size, there was a toilet and shower room and she had a small TV, there was a double bed in the corner and a closet, It was a bit like a large bed sit. It would have been hard for a westerner to stay in such a place but the Thai's were used to it and seem quite happy living like it. This is something I came to understand and the next few months would become my most enjoyable times whilst in Thailand.

Mom, Lek's friend's sister was coming to stay, that meant there were four of us going to be staying in the room! I thought it was a squeeze before but having someone else stay; it was going to be tight. The three girls slept on the bed I would sleep on the floor, the floor was very hard at first but I got used to it. In the evenings we all used to play cards and watch movies on the TV, sometimes they were in Thai but they all had English sub titles, the Thai's used them to help them learn English. Whilst staying there I experienced my first taste of street food, I had never tasted it before as I had the impression it was unclean or dirty, I would always eat in restaurants. The girls talked me into it and I grew to love it, not because it was inexpensive because I really did love it. You could get a really good meal for about 60 baht and the taste was out of this world. My favorite was the noodles with pork balls in a soup, this was one of the cheapest at 20 baht (about 30p), they would have spices you could put in the soup which tasted wonderful.

The Thais don't cook much they eat out all the time; they have the very basics in their kitchens and bring most of the food in from the street stalls. As I thought about it, it made sense if you cook for many people like a food stallholder does, its going to be less costly for everyone than a family cooking for themselves. Also you get to eat food fresh from the markets each day and nothing goes to waste. At first it looks bad or unclean seeing people eat off small tables in the streets but they do this three times a day, how expensive would it be if they ate in restaurants all the time? They would not be able to do it, a bit like we couldn't. I thought eating in the street was a better way of doing things; Thai's don't need all the dishwashers, cookers and fridges. It's not that they don't have the money for such things as I first thought. The reality is things are set up in such a way as they simply don't need them, unlike us.

People eating on the streets in Bangkok

I spent the next three months going to the British club in the days and then going back to Lek's place in the evening, we would then eat out on the street and sometimes go for a drink or to a Thai bar or Bobby's, I felt calm and not stressed out at all for probably one of the very few times in my life.

England summer 2004: I had flown back to England as my mate Karl was getting married; it was to be a posh affair at a stately home just outside the city. I was pleased for him as he had finally found a woman to settle down with. I planned to stay in the UK for a couple of months and decided to get a job, any job to get myself in a working frame of mind again. I come across an advertisement for a cleaner required at a pharmaceutical company called Pfizer's in Sandwich. I went for the interview and got the job.

I started almost immediately and was put on the night shift. I was to clean the offices, vacuum clean and polish desks. Although I hadn't done this kind of thing before apart from when I used to help my Granddad out when he was a caretaker at a school, I kind of got into it. It was easy work and I didn't have to think much although it was a bit physically demanding. I remember my first day and how big the place was, it was massive! Loads of offices and big offices not just with 10 or 20 desks in but large enough for 100's of desks, there was about 5 floors of these mega offices and that's only in one building. There is loads of buildings like this, some a mile long. They were all the same; it was easy to get lost in them. I didn't realise so many people were employed by pharmaceutical companies in offices, I thought there would be loads of laboratories and people making drugs, but this was not the case. The drug part of their operation was all robotic; all the drugs were made by machine! I started to think about why our pharmaceutical drugs are so expensive, I thought it was so they could pay off the large expense involved in trials and development. I started to doubt this and wondered if all these 10's of thousands of people employed in their flash

Aaron

offices had something to do with it. I mean how many people does it take to sell drugs? I had done very well on my own in the late 80's

I did this job for about a month then got sacked for eating in one of the offices; I was a bit upset as I actually really liked the job.

I returned to Bangkok as soon as I could. I had arranged to meet Jim and his new girlfriend at Bobby's Arms that evening for a drink. As soon as I got there Jim told me someone had put up a marquee next to Lumpini Park and the word about was they were going to do raves in it! He thought it was me because I had been investigating the idea of organising a party in a marquee before I left Bangkok a few months earlier. I was fuming as I knew I hadn't put up the marquee and knew from that point someone may be trying to copy my idea, but I hadn't told hardly anyone. Jim and David Quinne, the chairman from the British club were the only ones that knew about it. I knew Jim wouldn't say anything but wasn't sure about David. I decided to try and find out who it was for sure.

The next morning I went to the site of the marquee and found some guys working inside, I asked them who they were working for and they told me. It was some women who owned a local radio station and owned loads of businesses. I asked for her phone number and name and they gave it to me. I phoned the number and talked to her, I explained that I was from the UK and planning to do some parties in Bangkok and could we meet to discuss if we could be of help to each other. To my surprise she said yes.

We decided to meet that evening at Star Bucks coffee house just off Silom. I arrived early and waited and wondered what to say to her. I decided to come clean and tell her that I thought someone had stolen my idea and I wanted to know if she knew who.

A Thai lady walked through the door at about the time we arranged to meet; she looked very businesslike, I was sure it was her. I raised my hand and she walked over. "Hi" I said, she sat down. "You must be Aaron" she said, I said "yes". I still cannot remember her name but remember it was something western. I cut straight to the point and explained what I was planning to do in Thailand; she just smiled which can mean in Thai, I'm not saying anything. I decided to ask her what she was planning to do with the marquee", she said she wasn't sure yet! I wasn't getting anywhere. I asked her if she knew David Quinne from the British club but she just smiled again; I drank my coffee and said goodbye. At some point during the conversation she did mention she worked for a big company called Tero entertainment, I thought she was trying to scare me but didn't give it much thought until the next day.

The next day came and I decided to go and see her bosses, I was still fuming. I found a cyber café

Aaron

and proceeded to do a net search for a Thai company called Tero, I found a web site. The company was actually called BEC Tero and was massive. They organised concerts, had radio stations, owned venues and arranged televised sporting events in the city. At first I was impressed. Then I realised that the ventures BEC Tero were involved in were actually sub companies i.e. BEC Tero Exhibitions, and BEC Tero Radio and so on. I wondered what BEC was; I couldn't find out and presume it means Bangkok Economic Community. When I did a search I found a parent company called BEC World. BEC World had loads of sub companies like BEC Tero, at the time there was 20 of them. I understand there is a lot more now; Virgin Radio Asia is one of them. I then come across a financial statement which said BEC World was in fact a Plc and they owned more than 50% of all the sub companies' shares and all their sub companies owned more than 50% of their sub companies' shares. My heart stopped as I realised that the bosses at the top were in fact in control of all the companies and their sub companies right down to the bottom and my little idea of a rave in a marquee, just like one big pyramid! The fact escalated when I also noticed that a lot of the sub companies were media companies. I understand from Paul McKenna's writings and my own experience of how we can be controlled through this. I never thought there could be a business model like this, surely it was illegal as you could have one person controlling everything, I found their address and decided to go and have a nose around.

The address I got was on Sukhumvit a main tourist and business part of the city. When I got there I found the Emporium, this is a luxurious fashion and lifestyle shopping complex. Above this was a sky scraper consisting of hundreds of floors. I found all of the companies involved with BEC World in this building, you may think this is not strange but all the companies were placed on relevant floors in order of their place in the company, like a pyramid with BEC World at the top. I also found the Ministry of Education right in the middle of the building. I looked out the window whilst on one of the floors and saw a park next door. In the park was a large pyramid and I went down to have a look.

Aaron

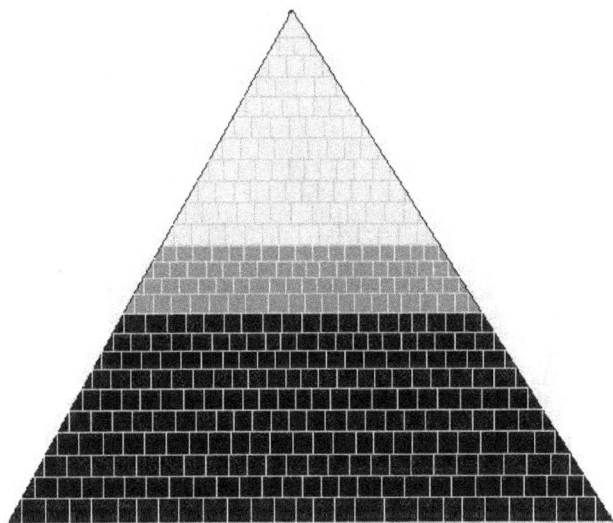

Aaron Phyall

BEC World Tower and the sculpture of a pyramid found in Benjasiri Park (Queens Park) Bangkok, Thailand

Aaron

Chapter 16 - Benjasiri Park (Queens Park)

I sat in the park for hours recapping what I had seen and what was going through my mind. There was a large tower in front of me; at the bottom was a large fashion, makeup and lifestyle shopping centre with loads of consumers going in and out buying stuff. Above this was a large TV, radio, entertainment, Media Company all controlled because a parent company (BEC World) who owns the majority stakes in them. In the middle was the ministry of education and I was sitting next to a large sculpture of a pyramid in a park. Call me paranoid but I thought there was something strange going on there, even the Thais were using this company to manipulate its population or they were trying to tell people something. I thought the latter of the two may be true, they had to have built this business model for a reason and I think it was so people could see. Then a plane flew over head and I started to think about the twin towers in New York. I had just thought previously they were offices that terrorists decided to take out but what if they consisted of a similar business model, like the one I was seeing in front of me. There could be loads of such models all around the world; it could even be standard business practise! Would this be a good reason for terrorists to target them? I know I didn't like the thought of it.

It was getting dark and I had been sitting in the park for hours when an old lady came over to me and offered me some Thai whisky. She was in her late 70's, dressed in old clothes and couldn't speak English, she was a street person, I took the whisky and drank with her. The next thing I knew was more street people came over and we all sat around drinking whisky, I asked about the pyramid but they didn't understand me as they only spoke Thai. One of them asked for money so I gave them some. They walked off and 10 minutes later came back with food, we all sat around eating it. I spent that whole evening in the park with them. At 10 o' clock the park keepers came and moved us on as they wanted to shut the gates, we moved outside onto the street and I stayed there all night with them drinking whisky and playing cards.

Morning came and I went back into the park, this time I noticed other sculptures placed in a big circle around a lake, there were about 15 of them, some carved in stone and others sculpted out of metal. I went and sat in front of the pyramid. The top was coloured gold, then in the middle it was blue and the bottom was black. It was about 20 feet in height and made up of small blocks like the ones that made up the pyramids of Egypt I had seen many years earlier. I decided to over lay the pyramid over the tower that was besides me in my mind, and found that BEC World was in the gold at the top, the Ministry of Education was in the blue in the middle and the Emporium was in the black at the bottom (see page 99). Surely this could not be a coincidence with all the other stuff I had noticed over the past 24 hours, I'm sure I wasn't just reading things into it. I then thought about why the Egyptians buried their pharaohs and queens at

Aaron

different levels in a pyramid, mainly at the bottom or in the black as it depicted in front of me. Well the emporium was in the black and I took that as being the consumers or common people or the people that were unaware of the blue and the gold above them. Could this be the class of people where the kings and queens of Egypt or maybe the future would come from? It was all getting a bit much for me I was starting to feel and sound mad.

I began to think about the kings and queens of the modern world and how they are figureheads and not actually in power. The kings and queens of Egypt in the past commanded their people, could the pyramids in Egypt be saying that there are modern kings and queens picked out from the common population (the black) to govern their people in the back ground. Is this why they buried their kings and queens at the bottom of a pyramid? My mind was in overdrive.

I spent the next few weeks just living in the park and thinking about the world, BEC World, Egypt and the pyramids. I was starting to feel unwell; my perception of the world had changed forever. I was over thinking but was I imagining all this, going mad or are we in fact being governed by some massive pyramid scheme? I decided to go to hospital and get myself checked out.

The Bumrungrad is the best private hospital in Bangkok, so I thought I would go there. They gave me a complete medical including blood works. They couldn't find anything physically wrong with me, apart from a low white blood cell count which is something I've always had. I decided to go back home to England.

Aaron

Chapter 17 - What is wrong with me?

Margate, England October 2003: I arrived at my parents. They had moved from Gravesend and now had this glorious flat overlooking Westbrook beach. My mum answered the door and was really please to see me, she hadn't seen me in a long time. She cooked me breakfast then I decided to get some sleep, I hadn't slept properly for weeks as I had been living in the park, also the journey home was long and tiring trip. It felt lovely sleeping on a soft bed that morning; I had the best sleep I'd had in months. That evening I awoke, my dad had got in from work and my brother Burma was also there. I remember trying to explain what I had found in the park in Bangkok, about the pyramid, BEC World and how I thought we could all be being manipulated but they couldn't understand what I was talking about. I decided to say no more about it and keep it to myself.

Over the next few weeks I became withdrawn, I didn't want to go outside and spent my days in my room just sleeping and thinking about Bangkok, looking out the window at the birds. I noticed how perfect they were and worried what we do to them; put them in cages and farm them intensively. As time went on things begun to get worse I start to get obsessed with turning the lights off to save power and only eating the minimal of foods. I had my reasons for this in my mind but to my family it was beginning to look as if I was acting bizarre. I would tell them we were all living in a business referring to the Tower and pyramid I had found in

Bangkok but they couldn't understand what I meant. In my mind at the time it was straight forward. I would look at the advertisements on TV, remember the media companies owned by BEC World and how they could be being used in Bangkok to make people purchase the goods in the Emporium below their offices. I got into a cycle of sleeping all day, I just shut myself off from the outside world, I didn't want to know. This went on all winter.

Spring came and my mother had brought a doctor to see me his name was Dr Cardigan, he knocked at my bedroom door and asked if he could come in, I said yes. I started to tell him of BEC World and how I thought it could manipulate us all, also that I thought the world was a business. He chatted to me for some time about these things and asked if I'd been doing street drugs, I said no, I hadn't touched drugs since Australia about 2½ years previously. He seemed genuinely worried about me. He then wrote me out a prescription and said I should take the drugs he had prescribed because I was depressed, if I did not I would get worse. He later left and I took the drugs for a few days then I stopped. I thought that the way I was thinking made a lot of sense but I couldn't see why no one else could see it. I felt so strongly about it I rewrote the lyrics of a song by David Grey and Five for Fighting (superman):

Aaron

We don't need to fly
I'm not that naive
I'm just out to find
The right side of things

We're not like a bird
We're not like a plane
We're more like some, sad old face inside a train
'Cos it aint easy too being free

I wish that I could cry
Fall upon my knees
Find away to die, in this life we're always lead.
It may sound absurd but don't be naïve
All us people have the right to bleed
I may be disturbed but won't you concede
All us people have the right to see
And it's not easy too being free

Stand up and portray how things should be
'Cos it's not right,
We can't all sleep sound at night
I'm not crazy,
or anything

We don't need to fly
I'm not that naïve
Men want men to ride
With clouds beneath their knees

I'm not like a monk, in a silly long sheet
Looking at dreams at night, on a one way street
only a monk, in a phoney long sheet
Is looking for special thing inside of we

Aaron Phyall

Inside of we
Inside of we
Yeah inside of we
Inside of we

I'm not like a monk, in a phoney long sheet
Looking at dreams at night on a one way street
I'm not like a monk, in a silly long sheet
And it's not easy
Oui. Oui, Oui
It's not easy
Too, be being free!

I spent the next few months sitting in my room, dodging visits from counsellors and various members of the crisis action team (CAT team) They were all trying to get me to take antipsychotic drugs, I couldn't see why I should as in my mind although I was distressed I felt I was thinking straight, I stayed in my room just thinking about things whilst painting and drawing pictures. I only left the flat on a few occasions. Things were getting stressful with my brother and parents, we started to argue and fight, I started to feel even more unwell, my concentration stopped again and I couldn't think, I was getting paranoid and getting mild hallucinations. Thinking back I was starting to feel like I did when I was on the course at AIGS in Bangkok. A doctor was called again by my mother but this time he brought a social worker and nurse with him.

Aaron

Chapter 18 - Sectioned

It was late one Friday evening at my parents when a nurse come into my room "can we speak with you Aaron", she said. "No" I replied, I just wanted to be left alone. She disappeared into the hallway, I could hear some talking. Then two men came in and introduced themselves, one was a doctor and the other a social worker. They said they wanted to admit me to hospital for a psychiatric evaluation and would I go with them. At first I said no but they managed to persuade me.

My Dad took me to Margate Mental Facility; we followed the doctor and social worker in the car. I got out the vehicle and proceeded to enter the automated doors into the building, my Dad walked beside me and we followed the doctor up the stairs. I noticed a sign on the wall saying Elmstone Ward. At this point I was quite relaxed and thought I would just talk to a doctor for an hour or so and then be allowed to go home. We entered the ward through a double door; I heard it lock behind me. In front of me was a large seating area with sofas, chairs and a small fish tank in the corner. At the far side of the place was an open door with another room full of people smoking, there was some shouting coming from it. A nurse come up to me and asked me to take a seat. It was at this point my father said he was going and would be back to see me tomorrow, I protested and said I wanted to go with him. "You can't, you have to see the doctor tomorrow" he said. I conceded to the fact that I would have to spend at least one night in the hospital. My Dad then left and promised to visit tomorrow. I cannot remember what happened next apart from the nurses offering me drugs; I refused them and was then later shown to my room. The rooms were small just consisting of a bed, closet and wash basin. There was a sash window which only opened a few inches, just enough to get your arms out. I went to sleep feeling duped into this situation, I never would have agreed to this if I had known they would be keeping me there all night.

I awoke the next morning not knowing where I was, I was a bit confused. I left my room and made my way down the corridor to the large seating area near the main doors. There were many people I passed on the way, some were just walking around, some were sitting down reading and others were arguing with nurses. I found it hard to cope with, I hadn't been around people in a long time, it all seemed a mass of confusion.

Through the far side of the seating room, next to the smoking room was the eating area which led onto the TV room. I made my way to the eating room and found a few people queuing up for breakfast. I joined the queue. Breakfast consisted of toast and marmalade, and various cereals, with tea or coffee. It was very bland but I ate it. I spent the rest of that Saturday morning sitting around the place waiting to see a doctor. Later that evening a social worker turned up his name was Melvin. Melvin was a cheery chap and full of energy, he took me into a room and we had a

Aaron

conversation. I cannot remember what we spoke of but I was probably very annoyed at having to spend the night in a psychiatric ward, I think a bit of shouting went on. Later I got to speak with a doctor, I didn't tell him about BEC World or about any of my other thoughts as I knew they probably wouldn't understand me as I had found this with a lot of other people so far. The doctor said I had to take my tablets or he wouldn't let me leave. I told him that I didn't think there was anything wrong with my thoughts and I wanted to go home. He said that I could go home after I had been taking some tablets for a while. This is the point when I realised they weren't going to let me leave that day. After the meeting with the doctor I tried to leave the ward, the doors were locked and I couldn't get out, the nurses informed me I had been sectioned. This meant I was locked inside for 28 days for observation, I protested but they said there was nothing they could do and that was the law!

I had made my mind up I was not going to take the tablets and knew from other patients they could not force me until after the 28 days of observation, then if a doctor, nurse and social worker agreed they could force me to take medication by means of an injection. Surely they would see I was sane in the 28 days, and have to let me go. I decided to wait for the 28 days section to finish.

Monday morning came and I noticed my name on the board in the sitting area, beside it was the name Dr Cardigan 10:30am, I recognised the name from my very first visit of a doctor at my parents flat 6 months before. He was to be my psychiatric doctor for my stay in hospital; I was to have ward round with him and his team every week.

10:30 came and I made my way to the TV room; this is where each doctor and there was a few of them, held their ward rounds every week on different days. Once in the room I noticed about 5 people sitting in chairs, there was another chair facing them, I presumed it was for me so I sat down. Dr Cardigan proceeded to introduce everyone "this is Dr Wheel" he said, he was Dr Cardigan's second in command a trendy looking guy in his mid 20's. "This is Sarah a staff nurse from the ward, she will be doing reports on how you progress on the ward, and you already know Melvin, your assigned social worker" he said. The other person was a student nurse who was just observing.

"So do you know why you are here Aaron?" Dr Cardigan said. At this time I was fuming I had been incarcerated here against my will and shouted "No, I haven't done anything wrong". "Its because you haven't been taking your tablets" he replied, "but there is nothing wrong with me" I said. I then proceeded to go into a long speech on how I had been duped into coming here and put on a section. Dr Cardigan then tried to explain I had a chemical imbalance in my brain and it had to be treated; he said I should take the medication. "What is the medication you want me to take" I

Aaron

said. "It's called Abilify, it's an antipsychotic and new out" he replied. I started to think of my time when I worked as a cleaner at Pfizer's and all of those 10's of thousands of office workers living off the proceeds of modern pharmaceuticals, I felt that they could be using the drugs to create jobs.
"How much does it cost?" I said, "I don't know" he replied, I had found out from a nurse that the dosage they wanted me on cost about £1000 a month at that time. I said no and refused to take the Abilify. The ward round ended and I stormed out.

I spent the next three weeks just trying to act normal, it was difficult as I had to be careful not to lose my temper after all I was being incarcerated against my will and virtually being blackmailed into taking neuroleptic medication, it was a difficult time. I must admit I began to experience sleepless nights and mild hallucinations and difficulty in concentrating as I had a few times before. I was beginning to see a pattern emerging and felt like this whenever I was in extremely stressful situations.

I found a computer in the occupational therapy (OT) room and spent hours doing drawings of stuff on it, it helped to pass the time and focus my mind. I designed some memorials and stone carvings, something which brought back memories of my time with Sam and the gang down at Medway Memorials, my old job. One evening Dr Wheel comes into the OT room to see me. I was drawing a picture on the PC of Benjasiri

Park (Queens Park) in Bangkok. I was just finishing off the main pyramid when he asked me what I was doing. I proceeded to tell him about what I had found there and how it puzzled me why the Egyptians buried their kings and queens at different levels of a pyramid. He told me I should take my medication and stop talking like that or they would have to inject me, he then disappeared out of the room. I started to feel stressed, over think and get mild hallucinations again. After some time I then had an assessment with a lady doctor. An hour or so later a male nurse come over to see me and said they needed to give me an injection, the 28 days were up and they had put me on a section 3, which allowed them to force medicate me. I refused.

The next thing I remember is a large group of nurses came storming in the room and grabbed me, they forced me down the corridor into my room. One of them had a needle in their hand, as soon as I saw it I started to fight. I was punching and head butting, pushing and shoving, there was blood on the floor. Then more nurses came in and finally overcome me, they injected me with a drug called Depixal. Afterwards I noticed a male nurse in the corridor with a noise bleed, it was one of them I had hit or head butted. I felt really guilty and apologised to him. I'm not a violent person but they did all pounce on me and injected me with a drug against my will.

I was starting to wonder what right did they have to force neuroleptic drugs into my body and brain,

Aaron

whatever was happening in my mind had happened naturally, so how could messing with chemical processes in my head fix this. Our bodies and brains are not stupid and given the right situation, I was starting to wonder if our brains could possibly fix themselves.

I would have to have these injections (depot) every 2 weeks and there was no way of avoiding it. I would have a few more confrontational incidents like this until I finally agreed to have the depot in an agreeable manner.

The weeks past and they kind of melted into one big one, every day was more or less the same, patients losing their tempers and throwing things, a lot of shouting, people coming in visiting, I kept myself to myself for a lot of the time. After a while I was granted leave which means you can go outside the ward. I was escorted at first but then allowed to leave the building on my own, it was only for a few hours a day, but it was something. I would spend most of my time at first in the hospital garden or walking down the paper shop.

I had been on the Depixal for about five weeks now, when I noticed I was having trouble walking, I begun to lose motor function in my legs, I felt all heavy and was getting blurred vision, I didn't feel well at all. Apparently or so I was told, I was getting some sort of toxic shock from the drug, it was horrible. I managed to persuade my doctor to put me on Abilify, the oral drug he was trying to get me to take at the beginning, he agreed. It meant I had to take a tablet every day without fail.

One Monday at ward round I asked Dr Cardigan if I could leave as I was now taking my medication and it had been about eight weeks since my admission. He said not yet as it takes a while for the new medication to work. I had discovered I could appeal my section and proceeded to do this and get a solicitor. Anna was the name of a solicitor I had chosen from a list the office staff had given me; she worked for a solicitor in my home town of Gravesend. I spoke with her on the phone and she said she would come and see me. I met with Anna the next day and explained the situation; she had a degree in forensic medicine as well as law. She said that talking to me she didn't feel I was psychotic in any way as she had met loads of patients that obviously were, I don't think she was saying this because she wanted the work, I felt there was nothing wrong with me too apart from I have slight strange episodes when introduced to stressful situations. We proceeded to put a case together. Anna proceeded to explain we would have to put our case forward to a tribunal, they would need a report from the nursing staff of the ward plus an evaluation from an independent doctor. She also said the Tribunal members are appointed by the Ministry of Justice and there are three of them. Anna went away and said she would be back the day of the hearing.

About three weeks past and I had finally got a date; my hearing was to be the end of that week. First a doctor turned up and interviewed me for

Aaron

about 20 minutes. I cannot really remember what we spoke about, it was probably the usual stuff like how are you feeling and are you still taking your medication. He then filled out a report on me and passed it on to the tribunal members. Anna turned up about an hour or so before the tribunal started and we went through what was going to happen. We then made our way down to a room on another ward, as we got to the bottom of the stairs I saw my parents and brother. I hadn't seen them for some time as I held them responsible for me being sectioned in this manner, and hadn't wanted them to visit me. I told them to go away as I thought this had nothing to do with them; they refused and said they were coming into the hearing. I immediately told my solicitor not to allow this and she made sure they were not allowed in. We went in the room and there were three people sitting behind a long table, they all looked very official. Then my doctor, Dr Cardigan came in and a staff nurse from the ward, they both sat down. My doctor then said how he thought I should remain in hospital as he felt my treatment was not yet complete. The nurse mainly said that they were happy with my progress now I was taking medication. Then my solicitor explained how I got sectioned and loads of other stuff I cannot quiet remember. They then asked me a few questions about how I was and where I would go if released etc. I tried to keep my answers short and I definitely wasn't going to say anything about BEC World to them! Although we were in the tribunal for about 30 minutes it all went very quickly and before I knew it they had said they would take me off my section. I was ecstatic; I walked out of that room with a big grin on my face. My parents were waiting outside and were angry as soon as they found out the news; my brother even threatened my solicitor! There was a commotion and loads of shouting, I just ignored them and went straight back to the ward. I stayed at Elmstone until the end of the week and then discharged myself one late afternoon.

I made my way to my parents flat, it was a cold night. I went to put my key in the lock but the door would not open. They had put the chub lock on so I couldn't enter. I didn't know what to do; I had nowhere else to go. I banged on the door but there was no answer. I decided to wait for someone to return.

About two hours past and I was sitting on the wall outside when I saw my mother walking towards me down the street. She just walked past me and went to enter the flat. "You've locked me out" I said. "Yes, you should still be in hospital you're not staying here" she replied and went into the flat. I then sat outside the place on the wall wondering. What did she mean I should still be in hospital, I had been taken off section by a tribunal and they had ruled I was deemed mentally fit. I was fuming, after all I had been through she still wanted me incarcerated. Who did she think she was some kind of a psychiatrist I was thinking? I hadn't seen much of her the past three months, in fact we had hardly spoke as I held her responsible for me being sectioned in the first place. I had found out

Aaron

while I was in hospital from my doctor that before I was admitted to a psychiatric ward she had repeatedly been phoning him up and trying to get me sectioned. Now I had just left hospital and with nowhere to go she had locked me out and left me sitting on the wall in the cold, I was starting to wonder if she was the one with mental health issues.

I continued sitting there all evening until my Dad arrived from work at about 10pm. He said I couldn't come in because it was causing problems with Mum. I said "where should I go?" He said I should go back to hospital, there is nothing wrong with me I protested why would I want to go to hospital, I was starting to feel stressed. I asked my father to get me my sleeping bag and coat from the flat, I would have to sleep on the streets. He went in and got my stuff and gave it to me, I left.

I didn't know what to do; I just felt I had to get away from that place. I had hardly any money on me and just the clothes I had on, I decided to walk. I walked along the esplanade and then the beach; I kept on walking until the beach stopped. By this time it was about 2am, there was nothing else I could do but walk. I ended up walking to Herne Bay about 20 miles away; here I found a train station. I looked at my watch; it was still early about 4am, so I curled up in my sleeping bag and waited for the early morning train. A train arrived around 6am and I got on it. I had no money on me and prayed a ticket inspector didn't get on. I was lucky one didn't and I stayed on the train all the way to Gravesend, my home town.

Once in Gravesend I just walked around, my old school, the old house I had with Sam in Whitehill Road, various parks I used to visit as a kid. It was troubling for the first time in my life I didn't know what to do or where to go. I continued mindlessly wondering around all day. I found myself at Riverview Park, a housing estate next to Gravesend, when I noticed a telephone box in the corner. I decided to phone my brother.

Burma was pleased to hear from me, I told him I was in Gravesend, he said to stay there and he would come and pick me up. He picked me up and took me back to my parents. I couldn't believe it when I arrived they were actually pleased to see me, nothing like the welcome I had got the evening previously. I went to my room and slept, I was tired. I spent the next few weeks at my parents flat and stopped taking the medication. I started to get really bad psychotic episodes, unknown to me I was about to be sectioned for the second time.

Aaron

Chapter 19 - St. Martins

There was a knock at the door, It was the police. My family and the doctors had decided I should be sectioned for the second time. The police come into my room and stood there all intimidating, the way only police can do. Arms folded and feet at a stance they informed me I was to get my stuff and an Ambulance would be coming for me.

The Ambulance turned up with three paramedics all dressed in green, just like on the TV program Casualty. I can tell you now I did not want to go with them, the police made it quite clear I had to. I got my stuff together, toothpaste, clean clothes and put them in a bag. By this time I am scared out of my whit's as I made my way down the stairs to the Ambulance with the crew and Police in tow.

Once in the Ambulance the crew assured me I would be okay, I was shaking like a leaf and scared out of my mind. It was a 40 minute drive to the mental facility in Canterbury, which was where they were taking me.

I felt the Ambulance slow down and drive over speed bumps, my heart was pounding, we had arrived at St. Martins Mental facility "You're okay" the paramedics kept saying, they were trying to reassure me. They could see I was distressed. The ambulance doors opened and two large male nurses appeared, dressed in white tops. They asked me to leave the ambulance. I left the Ambulance and followed one of them, the other one walked behind me. At the entrance to the ward there were two double doors, one of the nurses spoke into an intercom on the wall and the doors opened. We walked in. Opposite us there were another two double doors, as the doors behind us closed the doors in front opened, a bit like an airlock.

I remember, as I walked inside the main building I noticed a door on the left, It was open and I could see inside, there was a room. The walls of this room were all padded in a white cushiony fabric. I guessed it was a padded cell, just like you see in the movies. I was shitting myself. I prayed it wasn't where they were going to put me. We carried on past the room to my relief and to a seating area in the distance, "You can sit here and wait... you're okay" the nurses said. I sat down and waited. The nurses left.

I was sitting in the seated area on my own for about 10 minutes when female nurse approached me. She said we need to check you over and proceeded to take my blood pressure, I let her. Then another one approached with a large trolley with drawers and said she needed some blood. I thought about this and said no! I have a phobia towards needles you see. Also I have a theory I was starting to formulate that this only gives someone in a lab something to do, and creates jobs within the NHS, the doctors thought I was being paranoid. I had complete blood works done at the Bumrungrad hospital in Bangkok 18 month previously, when I first started to feel unwell; this

Aaron

never revealed anything wrong with me. The nurse walked off. The other nurse proceeded to take my blood pressure and said it was very high, I said, "well what do you expect, I've just been sectioned and bundled into an ambulance by the police!" she smiled and walked off. I didn't think it was very funny although she had a great smile; I was fuming about what had happened to me that evening but scared and shaking like a leaf inside.

The next thing I knew was my parents and brother Burma were walking down the corridor towards me; this made me even more annoyed for they were the ones who had instigated me being sectioned again that night in the first place. I cannot remember what exactly happened next there and then but we had a big argument about how they had treated me the past few days. I thought they were out of order especially after I had only just been released from my first admission from a psychiatric ward. My brother was saying something about me saying to him previously that we could all be living in a computer and this is why he thought I was mad; this is something which I had said but didn't totally agree with. There was a small element in my mind that wondered if it could at all be possible. "So what are we all living in then?" I commented to him, there was no answer. Because of the shouting and disruption to the ward the nurses asked them to leave.

A nurse showed me to my room. The rooms at St. Martins were quite nice, large and spacious. Not like Elmstone ward in Margate. The nurse offered me a sleeping tablet with a glass of water, I couldn't convince myself to take it, I said no. The nurse left and I proceeded to put my things away and get undressed. By now I was beginning to calm down and getting used to the fact I was going to be spending 28 days here, under a section 2 this was the amount of time given to the doctors to make an assessment of me, if they want to after the 28 days they could put me on a section 3 which is for 6 month, then after this it's a year's contract! And you never get out. I had one last chance before I got caught up in this spiralling cobweb of hospital incarceration and forced medication. At the moment they could only hold me for 24 hours I had to convince a doctor and social worker in the morning I was in a fit mental state, if not I would be on a section 2 and thought all would be lost. I slept.

The next day I had an interview with the house doctor and social worker, I tried my best to act sane and I think I did, apart from losing my temper a few times at being held against my will. It was no good though, they weren't going to let me go, my worse thoughts were confirmed and they put me on a section 2. I then spent the next few weeks at St. Martins until they transferred me back to Margate and Elmstone ward.

Once back at Elmstone I was feeling rough I cannot remember large parts of my admission there, it was like I was in a different world. I was getting what I now call fading, I would look at

Aaron

someone and it was as if two people were blending into one. I would look at them speaking and see two lips overlaying one another, it scared me. After a while they got me back on medication and I started to feel better. I would go on to stay in Elmstone ward for about six months, all over Christmas and well into the following year. I thought they would never release me. But then one day in ward round my doctor said I was well enough to leave but I needed to find a place to stay. They advised me not to go back to my parents and to get a place of my own. I eagerly found a holiday flat in Ramsgate to use as my address. I did this only to get myself out of hospital as I had enough and decided to leave the country and get away from it all as soon as I had been discharged.

Chapter 20 - Back on the Road

I landed back in Bangkok around May, thinking back that's the worse place I could have gone, a hot muddled city full of loud noises, memories of the past like BEC World that had first made me ill, I had come off my tablets and only lasted about four weeks, I returned to the UK in a right mess, my psychotic episodes were getting worse. I got admitted to hospital again and spent the next Christmas at Elmstone ward in Margate. It was then I realised I would now probably have to take tablets every day for the rest of my life.

A process of years travelling abroad and then hospitalisation on my return happened even when I was taking the medication. Each time I returned messed up and the doctors increased my dosage. I went back to Thailand and then Kenya and Tanzania trying to start my gemstone business but I eventually got ill and had to return prematurely. I never thought I would be in a position to work again I was gutted. I had made good contacts for Tanzanite and Tsavorite (a green garnet) at source in Africa, I only had to get the stones to my contacts in Bangkok to make a good profit. I just couldn't do it; I kept getting ill. I was taking the medication so why was I getting sick? Then I started to realise it may be because I was putting myself in stressful situations, my mind and body just could not handle it. I decided to try and reduce my stress loads the next time I travelled.

Aaron

2007 Julius and I talking gemstones at a secret location in Tanzania, Africa

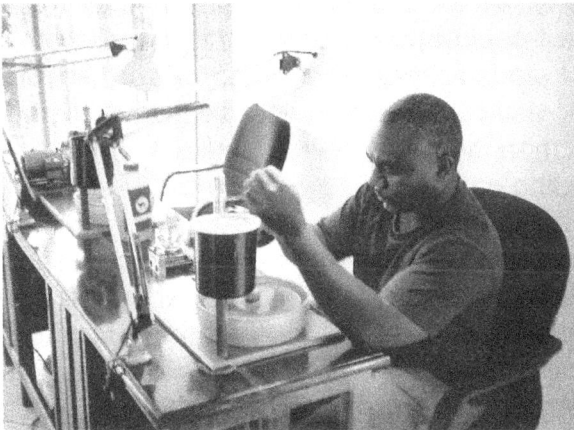

Julius faceting Tanzanite at a lapidary table in Tanzania, Africa

Aaron Phyall

March, Heathrow airport 2008: I had left Margate at 5:30am on a train to London. I was to get a flight to Bogota, Columbia via Miami. I was going on a recognisance mission to find Emerald dealers and miners from the north of the country.

Heathrow was ramo with people, it normally was but the last few years had got worse. They had implemented new security checks to try and combat publicised terrorism. After collecting your ticket from the airline front desk you have to make your way through security. This now takes ages as they check nearly everything and everyone, if your unlucky you even have to remove your belts and shoes and have them x-rayed. All those people pushing and shoving, I was starting to feel a bit uneasy. When I got through I found the quietest place I could and sat down and had something to eat. I stayed there for an hour or so then made a quick visit to boots to buy a disposable camera. It was then time for me to make my way to the boarding gate.

I boarded the plane for my first leg of the journey to Miami. It was a long flight of about 10 hours; I watched a couple of films and then tried to sleep for the rest of it. It was difficult as I had put on a lot of weight with the medication and this made the seats seem quite small. I reached the predestination of Miami on a bit of a non eventful flight, I didn't really get speaking to anyone and the air hostesses were all ugly. At Miami I had to queue for about 2 hours just to get to the transfer lounge as American security insisted on taking

Aaron

everyone's finger prints, I nearly missed my connection! Once finally on the connecting flight to Bogota things were a lot better the plane was only half full and the flight was only 4 hours, I began to relax. I reached Bogota at about 10pm and disembarked the aircraft. I then made my way through passport control and on to collect my suitcase. It all went smoothly up until then and I was surprised at how efficient everything was at Bogota's airport. I then discovered they had lost my suitcase and they thought it was left in Miami, it didn't make the connection. They were very apologetic and said they would bring it to the hotel I was staying at tomorrow evening. I was annoyed but refrained from losing my temper as my main goal on this trip was to avoid stress. I went through customs without any problems and proceeded to change some money into Columbian pesos. I then went to the taxi office outside the airport and gave them the address and name of my hotel. They printed a piece of paper out in Spanish for the driver and give it to me. I jumped in a cab and headed for the hotel.

I had decided to stay in the old part of the city at a hostel called Platypus. It wasn't really a hostel of type but more like a low grade hotel. By this time I was getting a bit stressed as it had been a long journey, I was also worried what I was going to find here in Columbia as I've heard some bad things about the place on the TV. I arrived at Platypus at about 11:30pm and proceeded to check in.

From the outside the Platypus hotel looked like a row of houses from the TV program Coronation Street but on a hill, once inside it was quite large. There was a security gate after you got through the front door, which was opened electronically from the office, a bit like the entrance to the mental hospitals I was admitted to back home. A small court yard where people sat around talking and drinking was in front of me, off to the side, were various rooms, one with a television in and others containing a kitchen and tables for eating and socialising. At the back were the bedrooms.

I made my way to the office and introduced myself and told them I had made the booking from home on the internet. They had been expecting me and had a room in Platypus 2 just up the road ready for me. One of the staff asked me to follow them. We walked outside and proceeded up the hill.

Platypus 2 was the exact same layout as Platypus 1 but in need of some work, the walls needed repainting and there was an old feel about the place, I wasn't bothered though as I had stayed in worst places, I just wanted to get some rest. My room was at the back of the place next to a small courtyard. The staff member left and I decided to get some sleep.

Aaron

Platypus Hostel Bogota, Columbia

I awoke the next morning to the sound of a male English accent; it was coming from the courtyard. I popped my head out the door and noticed two guys talking, one was an American in his late 20's, the English guy was in his late 50's. The English guy's name was Peter and he said "hi, do you fancy a line of coke" I hadn't had any for years and promptly said "yes", they both then made their way over to my room. I invited them in and Peter proceeded to line three up on the desk in front of me. He took the white powder from a small plastic bag with a knife he pulled out of his pocket; the cocaine I was use to having back home was yellow. He then placed it on the table and proceeded to cut it up into a fine powder. Then three small lines were made. Dan the American guy had already rolled up a note and he passed it to me, I immediately stuck the note up my nose and put my head down towards the white powder, I then sniffed as hard as I could. I could feel the coke beginning to run down the back of my throat. I was starting to feel the freeze and my throat going numb, I then handed the note to Peter. After about 5 minutes I began to feel very relaxed and confident, I had no rushes or sweating like you get with the gear back home, I just felt very in control. We chatted normally for about half an hour and then had another line. This was a coke buzz I had never had before it was mild; it didn't make your brain race and was quite mellow. I hadn't felt like this before on coke. I asked Peter where he had got it, and he said from the locals," it's the coke they do" he said. He had paid £3 for the gram and said that was expensive for Columbia, he could get me some this evening if I liked. We spoke for another half hour and then I decided to go out and try and score myself. Before I left I met a young traveller in the TV room, he said there was an African guy that stands on the corner by the shops just over the back serving up coke. I decided to go and see if I could find him.

I found the shops and on the corner where the traveller said, just by a food vender's shop was a tall African guy with a baseball hat on. I

Aaron

approached him and said "have you got any gear",
he said "what you looking for coke", I sad "yes".
He said to follow him around the corner and
proceeded to pull out a fist of small plastic bags
full of a white powder. "Its 10,000 pesos a gram"
he said, I said "give me 50,000 worth" (about £15)
he did and handed me some bags, five grams in
total. I made my way back to Platypus and my
room. I wondered why it was white and thought it
may be cut with something and been repressed. I
decided to make it into crack so I could see how
pure it was. I was surprised as I got a return of
80%, it hadn't been cut! This had to mean it was
from a natural cocaine plant and not a cloned
hybrid designed in a lab, which is the sort of
powerful coke we get in the UK. I spent the next
week smoking and sniffing my purchase until it
had all gone. If I had done this back home with our
stuff it would have taken me a week to get over
the ordeal but here in Columbia I felt fine.

I would spend my days relaxing, going to coffee
shops, walking around the city and talking to
travellers at the Platypus. It was very calming and
I felt de-stressed. Bogota is like any other city I've
been to apart from there wasn't congested traffic
like I had expected; the buses and cars seemed to
flow in an orderly manner. It had markets with
street vendors and parks with students sitting
around reading books, grand stone buildings
amongst limestone paved courtyards, loads of
people walking around during the day getting on
with their business. As night came they would all
disappear and the city would turn into a bit of a

ghost town by 10pm. I never worked out where they all went but presumed back to their homes and families. I did see poverty and people living on the streets but no more than in any other major city I'd been to. This wasn't the Columbia I had been expecting, I had seen news reports and documentaries on the violence and drug culture that was supposedly rife in Bogota back home. I never saw any of this during my visit and would go as far as to say it was a safe city. After a week I decided to make my way up north to the mountains to look for the Emerald mines, miners and dealers.

I had worked out the easiest way to get to the mines which were located about 200 miles north of the city. I would make for a small town called Muzo which nestled on the edge of the Emerald belt high up in the Andes. I got a cab to the bus station and from there a coach up north to a town called Cipaquira. The journey lasted about 2.5 hours. On the way I passed lakes and farms and lush green forests, the views were stunning. From Cipaquira I had a wait of about an hour and then a 4 hour trip in a 4X4 through mountain passes and escarpments. On this leg of the journey the 4X4 was stopped twice by armed soldiers. On both occasions I was searched and so was the vehicle, they were looking for drugs and weapons. I was lucky I hadn't bought any coke with me and had consumed it all back in Bogota.

Aaron

The Columbian Army searching our vehicle for cocaine and guns

I arrived in Muzo late evening and booked in a hotel just across from where I was dropped off, the journey had taken about 8 hours from Bogota and I was tired but still decided to have a quick look around the town before I slept. It was about 10pm and the place was deserted, there were a few pool halls still open but very few people in them. I found a bar which was just shutting up and tried to get a drink, but they were closing and weren't going to serve me. I walked back to the hotel and decided to have an early night.

When I awoke the next morning I made my way down to the reception, I was greeted by a load of

Emerald dealers who had found out there was a buyer in town. I spent the whole of the morning going through parcels of rough and cut Emerald, looking for samples to take home to show my contacts. Most of the stuff was of low quality and for the tourist market but I did meet a man who said he was a gem cutter and he had a lapidary business just down the road. I decided to visit him in the afternoon.

Everything in Muzo revolves around a main square; you have a small police station in the corner, some shops and small businesses selling various goods. I made my way there and had lunch. While sitting at a table the gem cutter I had met earlier passes me on his motorbike, he stopped just across the square. He then beckoned me to come over. I left my lunch and went over to him and he proceeded to go into a workshop. I followed him in. Once inside I could see a lapidary table with various polishing equipment on it. He was speaking to me in Spanish as he didn't speak English, I don't speak Spanish so we proceeded to have a conversation using crude sign language. He pulled out of his pocket a pair of Emeralds; they were cut in the traditional emerald cut and were about 4 carets in size each. I looked at them using my loupe and then under sunlight outside, they were natural. They were truly beautiful and of a wonderful rich dark grass green colour, they had inclusions but that is only to be expected with Emeralds anyway. When asked, he said he wanted $1000 for them; I was amazed I could get $800 plus a caret for them back home. I wanted to buy them but only had £300 in sterling on me and about £200 in pesos. I asked if he would take sterling but he said no only pesos or US dollars. The only bank in Muzo didn't change money and there wasn't an ATM! I was gutted I couldn't buy them. I hadn't taken much money with me as I hadn't intended to purchase many Emeralds on this trip as I was worried about getting robbed and thought I would leave this until I new the score. This was entirely meant to be a fact finding mission to get contacts and work out prices. I had planned to visit again on a buying trip later in the year. I ended up spending the £200 in pesos on some samples from a miner I met the next day. I spent only 3 days in Muzo and wasn't able to get to the mines as you have to be invited to go there by a local. I did meet some contacts there and am confident I will get to see the mining operation and purchase some quality stones on my next visit.

A Miner selling me Emeralds at the square in Muzo, Columbia

I made my way back to Bogota and the Platypus hotel. I spent my remaining few days there just chilling in the city. There was a concert on in the main square and I got to listen and watch Columbian musicians, they were quite good but nothing compared to the Thai's I had seen playing in Bangkok.

On my return I thought of what I had seen and learned of Columbia, it was a beautiful city and country, the people were most friendly. The

Aaron

cocaine although pure was nothing like we get in the UK, it was of a mild and natural strain, I did not get the urge to do more after my first purchase of the drug and believe it helped chill me out and focus my thoughts. I learned that the locals (Andeans) had been using the coca leafs since the times of the Incas as anaesthetics and to help heal the body and focus the mind. I was surprised to learn I could get cocaine for as little as £1 a gram in Columbia if I bought it in bulk. The neuroleptics I'm on at the moment are costing about £30 a day! They both have side effects but believe me the ones you get with cocaine in small doses are a lot less than modern neuroleptic drugs (see Chapter 21.). I had no psychotic episodes on my return and fell into normal life okay. I'm sure the reason I was okay on this trip was because I took it easy and had less stress but do wonder if it had anything to do with the cocaine I took. I will be able to tell later in the year, as I'm back off to Africa where cocaine is not available.

Chapter 21- Gemstones can wait!

Margate, summer 2008: I had decided to spend some more time in this country and try and rekindle the long relaxing and stress free summer times of my youth. Back then they seemed to go on forever, beaches long rides in the countryside, hop farms and light sunny evenings in pub gardens. This is something that I had not experienced for a long time due to travelling and incarceration in various psychiatric wards. I decided to buy a motorbike and spend some time exploring the winding traffic free country lanes of the area. Gemstones can wait! I remember thinking.

The motorbike I bought was a Superbyke RMR a Super Moto and all painted in a mat black. It was made in China and the latest model, it really looked the business. I was worried about the quality of the vehicle at first as rumor had it in the motor trade that China had a reputation of putting out some cheap crap. A worry that soon faded as I realised my new purchase was the best and the ride was as good as any other bike I had ridden over the years, if not better. I quickly realised China had built something which was designed to be value for money, safe and last a realistic number of years. Some parts were copied from older proven models of Japanese and British bikes, maybe because parts of these bikes have passed the test of time and not because they wanted to rip off other manufactures. Was China just trying to make money? I wondered, or were

Aaron

they in fact trying to build something which they enjoy doing, was economical to make, looks good, lasts and would be of help to everyone who needed one. Traits which I have come to respect in any business or country. My mind was put at rest during the Beijing Olympic Games, China really knew what it was doing and for the benefit of its people and customers alike. Now in a sense, I see it as if they are looking after us by making a lot of our goods cheaper and well priced, not trying to make money from us as countries have tried to do in the past. I felt the smallish UK shopkeepers had been getting greedy on their mark-ups of imports and taking the cash for themselves. Although I felt this was changing as we can now bypass them on most things, because we have the Internet.

I would spend the sunny days navigating the country lanes on the RMR, it made me feel seventeen again and I remembered the times before I had started my working life, times which were not stressful, uncomplicated and kind of free. I thought it would be a good idea if I tried to recreate elements of my youth and throughout my life which made me feel happy and balanced in my thoughts. To do this I would have to write parts of my life story down so I could pick out these elements and also bits which could help me identify what has gone wrong with me. I set about on a four week mission to do this and found myself sitting at the computer each day typing frantically at the keyboard, thinking back into the past. I would take various breaks during the day and disappear on my motorbike to a string of hotels and cafés along the coast front, Viking Bay in Broadstairs was a favorite place of mine. I would sit on the cliff tops in the gardens of the hotels and restaurants with a coffee, smoking cigarettes and reading through printed off copies of the manuscript I had written the day before. I was amazed at the amount of stuff I had remembered and managed to write down, although a little disgusted at the bad things I had done in my life. It was very therapeutic for me and I started to feel as if I was beginning to know myself at last. After about four weeks I had just about finished writing and decided to go through some old photos I had in my flat. I placed them in the word document I had written and then printed the lot out.

I was telling someone about what I had done a week or so later and they told me about 'Chipmunka Publishers', a publishing firm that publishes books to do with a new Genre of books, 'Mental Health'. I looked at their website and decided to send them a copy of what I had written. A week later I got an email saying they were prepared to publish my manuscript as an eBook. I was surprised but also excited and worried at the same time. What would people think of me? The drug consumption and dealing, criminal activities and my deepest private thoughts all written down for them to read, my psychiatrist doesn't even know these things! All this stuff which I had managed to so far keep private and a secret in my life. Should I change the manuscript or delete certain parts? To protect the way people now see me today and people I had been associated with. I decided that because I had done these things and although regretted doing a lot of them, these experiences have made me the person I am today, which I consider to be a relatively nice one although a bit distressed at times. I had spent a lot of time remembering my past while writing and what I had written was all true, if people were to read it I wanted them to hear my true story.

I negotiated a contract with 'Chipmunka' and signed on the dotted line. I then sent the publishers the original version with a couple of added chapters and they then published it in eBook format.

I read my manuscript from cover to cover quite a few times over the next few weeks. I could finally identify what made me happy and what made me stressed-out and sad. I found Materialistic things like big houses; cars and flashy gadgets didn't make me happy for very long, I decided not to buy anymore of them. Weddings and anywhere I was on display made me stressed including chaotic cities, I decided to never go there again. Marriage and divorce made me really sad; I knew this already and had decided years ago to never do it again. What made me happy? Thai street food, Sun, scuba diving, gemstones and travelling. I thought about making Thailand my base in the future, somewhere out of the city of Bangkok in the Gulf of the country. I could scuba dive whilst there and there is a lot of Sun and fresh Thai street food. Gemstones could continue to be my choice of future career and income, I decided to travel the non-stressful places of the world and look for gemstones for the rest of my working life. It all sounded very nice! But could I manage to make it all happen?

I now found it so easy to identify most of the key points in my life which made me happy, stressed and sad because I wrote the eBook. It had triggered all my old memories and I could now remember all the things from most of my life. The only thing I had to do now was get off the medication I was being made to take. I was on 15mg of Abilify a day at that time. This is quite a low dosage for anyone on neuroleptics, I was lucky and just about able to get away with refusing to take a higher dose from the doctors. I had learnt that you have to be careful when coming of these dugs in previous attempts and experiences as your mind sees it a bit like Heroin; it's grown to need it. You have to come off it slowly or you end up in a right mess. I now know one of the main reasons my mind got all confused and I got sectioned on some of the previous times was because I just stopped taking the pills all at once. I knew there was a good chance I could get sectioned again this time although I was being careful. I was apprehensive but understood it was the only way forward for me. I had made my mind up I was not going to stay on the medication for the rest of my life for reasons I will explain in the next chapter. I dropped my dosage by 5mg and planned to take the remaining 10mg for the rest of

Aaron

the summer. To reduce the dosage even more I would have to get rid of all the remaining stresses in my life. I felt my family caused a lot of them especially my mother, I decided to get rid of her! How would I do this? Should I kill her? The thought bounced around my head for a while but I then realised this was not an option after about 2 days of playfully considering it! I would just have to get well away from her while I was coming of the tablets.

I needed somewhere close to the UK, somewhere which was relatively stress-free and scuba diving was available. Also somewhere there was a lot of sun in our winter and was inexpensive as I had not been well enough to make much cash over the past five years. I still had some reserves but I needed it to buy gemstones when I was fit and ready. The only place I knew that was close was Egypt. I decided to spend our winter coming of my medication there.

Although Egypt met most of my needed qualities all of its cities I had been to were stressful, I decided to venture to a place right on the coast and far south of Cairo on the west side of the Red Sea, it's called Hurghada. I had been there before with Sam (my x-wife) about 20 years previous on my first trip East from the UK and to Egypt. Although it was run down at the time we were there, the place did have a small harbour but from what I remember was a bit too manic of a town for me at this time. I had heard things had changed though and the place has been rebuilt, it was now more of a resort for European holidaymakers. It is of apparent foreign design and finance or so I have been told. New buildings and hotels are scattered all around the coast. I imagined a large chilled out place, not boring, a place where I could get by without sign language and just speaking English, a perfect place to relax get off the medication and in a hot sunny climate! The Sun always tended to make me feel happy. I scoured the Internet for reasonably priced flights and found a return for £200; I booked the flight leaving at the beginning of November. I spent the rest of our summer and autumn chilling out, going to the beaches, coffeehouses, rewriting my eBook and adding content for a paperback version. I would ride my RMR throughout the country lanes and continue to take my reduced dosage of Abilify, 10mg. It was a bit like being retired.

I felt fine during the above period although a bit bored and lonely. Most of my friends I had from the old days had families now and were doing their own thing. The mates I had made travelling were all far away and I started to wonder if I needed a woman in my life again to help complete my planned recovery.

I had met quite a few women over the years and on my travels most of which I have decided not to write about, maybe because I never got that close to most of them like I did with Sam and Lek. Most of them wanted babies, money or just large houses with a mega mortgage, a road I have not been prepared to go down in my later years and

Aaron

believe I never will again. I began to realise though I would have to find a woman at some point in my life to be with for my mental state at least as being on my own would drive me mad in itself. I had decided many years ago I would never get married again and fall into the trap of trying to start a family, after all the lot of it is only hormonal driven and is bound to wear off on me at some point in the future. I have known from an early age that if you think with your head instead of your hormonal emotions when contemplating babies a lot of us would choose not to have them. After all this is not a nice world to bring children into at the moment although things do seem to be improving globally. Also the way things are setup on this planet at this time, if you have kids they are going to be really expensive for you and restrict you. Once you have committed yourself you're probably fucked financially for most of your life. Having said all this though dying alone didn't seem that appealing to me either!

I was starting to feel depressed with all the thinking; could it be because of the 5mg drop in medication? I wondered, I had finished planning the next year of my life in my mind and decided I should continue with the 5mg drop but try and cheer my miserable self up! Before I left for Egypt.

September came and it was my 38th birthday. I tried not to think about it too much but the fact was I was getting old. The past 5 years had flown by and I hadn't really accomplished that much, not like in the previous 10 years when up till then I had done a lot for someone of my age. The main reason for me slacking was I had spent half of those 5 years in psychiatric wards and what with the different kinds of neuroleptics I had been on; I felt these things had dampened my spirit. I was trying but all the enthusiasm in me was disappearing so I decided to try and make myself go out to the bars and clubs at the weekend and just enjoy myself.

It was no good though I just found myself sitting at the bar drinking and drowning my sorrows. I spent a lot of time in the Mechanical Elephant with my brother Burma, a pub on the sea front but just ended up talking to the odd local about depressing things like why no one visits Margate anymore. Having the RMR was helpful though and I continued ridding it around the local area, it really cheered me up.

October came and so did the end of our summer. Looking back I suppose it was okay, nothing like I had hoped and although we did have a few sunny weeks it seemed far removed from those long, free summertime's of my youth I was trying to recreate. I did do a lot with my time though, a lot more then I did in the previous few years but things were beginning to get mundane and I was finding things a little bit boring.

I had 4 weeks until my flight left for Egypt so although I was feeling a little down in the dumps I decided it was time to reduce my medication yet again. I dropped the dosage of Abilify by another

Aaron

5mg, which left me taking half a tablet a day (5 mg). If I wasn't getting any psychotic episodes by the end of the month I felt I would be okay to come off the remaining 5mg whilst in Egypt.

I spent the remaining month before my trip getting the correct scuba gear together. I had decided to buy the equipment as I would be diving twice a day whilst in Egypt and renting gear that doesn't fit properly can be uncomfortable. Also purchasing something seemed to give me a bit of a feeling I was starting to accomplish things again. I found a great website on the Internet which sold anything to do with water sports and promptly ordered a shit load of stuff. When it arrived I eagerly tried it all on and spent a few hours walking around the flat in it. The wetsuit was a bit tight as I had ordered a large knowing I was probably and extra large but hoped as I was coming of the medication I would loose weight quickly.

November came and I was taking my reduced dosage of 5mg of Abilify. I was starting to find it difficult to sleep and my mind was racing .It was the weekend before I was due to leave for Egypt and I found myself yet again at Canterbury psychiatric hospital talking to the house doctor, I cannot remember how I got there but knew I had been awake for three days. "I cannot sleep" I said to the doctor, "have you stopped taking your medication again" the doctor said to me. I didn't want a lecture on why I should take medication so I didn't answer his question then proceeded to tell him how I hadn't been able to sleep for the past few nights and this was why I thought I was getting a psychotic episode. The doctor then proceeded to admit me to the ward for an evaluation. Although I was admitted voluntary, which meant I was legally free to leave the ward if I chose, the doctors made it quite clear if I tried to leave then they would section me! I was stuck in a psychiatric ward yet again and just as I was due to leave for Egypt, I was gutted as my plan had failed; they wouldn't let me leave and go on my recovery trip to Egypt.

A standard procedure then followed of me refusing sleeping tablets and various assortments of psychiatric drugs. In the end I had no choice but to comply and take them, after a week I was back on the pills and was sleeping again although it was artificial sleep and induced by powerful medication. I did start to feel better and the psychotic episodes stopped. I managed to get away with only taking the minimal of drugs whilst in hospital this time and was discharged after only six days; this was far removed from the four to six months stints I had been incarcerated for in previous years, I was thankful.

December 2008: On discharge from hospital I had some good news at last from my publishers. The eBook was doing great on the web-site and they said they wanted to print it in paperback for the New Year. I was pleased about this but had hoped to finish this story on a more of a happy note, In Egypt off the medication and back on track in my life and career but the fact is I'm still on the pills

Aaron

and struggling to keep things together, I do feel better than I have in previous years but ironically for now I'm still not able to live without being involved with drugs! Because I have to take the Abilify every day!

So what of the future I wonder the gemstones and my planed move to Thailand's Gulf Coast? Gemstones and Thailand will wait... I'm thinking!

A top Tanzanite crystal 17.2 carats sourced from the 'Blue Mountains', Tanzania, Africa

Chapter 22 - On Reflection (stuff that's been bouncing around my head)

Are we the money?

Margate England Present day: If all the money in the world was divided up evenly then everyone would have a dollar a day to live on! That's what John had said to me in Bangkok that New Years Eve years previously (*Chapter 15*). I had back then believed that money was backed up by gold as most of us do but could it be backed up by people? I decided to try and work it out and this is what I found.

This is difficult to get your head round and I'm not sure as I totally have yet but here are my thoughts anyway.

First to work this out you have to understand what a trillion is. In America for some reason a billion is 1,000,000,000 (a thousand million) but in the UK a billion is 1,000,000,000,000 (a million million), we shall use the UK billion and keep it in dollar format; this will help get round the US and UK billion problem. We will also use America as an example: The world has approximately 2.55 UK Trillion dollars a year in money (7 billon people in the world x 365 Days of a year). America has about 8 trillion US dollars in the M3 money supply (0.8 UK Trillion dollars) according to the Internet. This includes all the cash in the country plus money in banks: including travels checks, moneymaking funds and CD's. That's about 7.3 X their UK 0.11 trillion dollar allocated money per year (305 Million people in the USA x 365 days of a year). So where is all the extra 0.69 UK Trillion dollars coming from? Well they must be taking it or borrowing it from somewhere. I would like to think the latter is true and they are borrowing it but how can you borrow something which someone simply just don't have; after all the world only has 2.55 Trillion a year to live on, where is the extra coming from; Another planet? This would not surprise me if they were already trying to do this! The fact is they are borrowing or taking it from somewhere and I think it is the third world countries. These people are mostly living on a lot less than a US dollar a day. If we are the money then surely we should all have about 1 UK dollar a day to live on.

Where is all the money going?

Another important point to highlight in the above American case is where is the extra 0.69 UK trillion dollars going? This is a question that has bothered me and the only answer I can come up with is: The Americans are spending it mostly on themselves on travel and transit, food and building materials, clothes and entertainment, with some aid relief. This is something that people in the third world countries simply don't all have because the Americans have taken or borrowed their share of it from them. After all people in third world countries may be part of the money as we all may be. We could all be roughly equal, i.e. 1 person = 1 UK Dollar a day.

It's not just America that may be doing this but the whole of the developed world although to different extents. No wonder Africa and places like Burma are in such a state!

To help me try and understand where all the money is going in the world I have tried to look at the past in the UK. The old people and History tell us that they didn't have the choices or things we do in the UK today, especially things like travel, clothing and foods. Years ago travel is something we know everyone just did not do, they tended to stay and work in their home towns and did not fly around the world, food was only available from the country i.e. there was no fresh foods like bananas or apples and meats coming in from half way across the globe. I have noticed in some countries this is still the case, especially Thailand. The reason Thailand doesn't do this in my opinion is the same as why our great grand parents did not, because it's expensive (it costs a lot of people). Today in the UK we are free to travel the globe on planes and travel 100 miles to work each day by cars, trains or on the buses. You could say it's because the population has gone up, there is more of us to build and maintain these things or we now have more technology but Thailand has about the same population and is about the same size as the UK. They have the technology but still choose not to do this, they remain independent as a country for food and clothing, just like we once did. This leads me to think that although it sounds cheap for us now in this country to fly practically anywhere in the world for just £600 or buy a bunch of bananas all the way from Africa for just £1.20, it actually cost a lot more than this and in people or peoples standards of life elsewhere. We could be being subsidised by the third world for our standards of living and luxuries.

Sectioned

I realise the doctors and nurses thought they were helping me by injecting me that very first time (Chapter 18), but what right did they have to force neuroleptic drugs into my brain, drugs which they admit to not totally understanding how they work. Yes I was acting strange, hallucinating and probably coming out with things they couldn't understand but whatever happened in my head had happened naturally so a natural solution was required to fix my thoughts, if they did indeed need fixing at all. The way I see it now is how could meddling with the chemical processes in a brain improve things for the better in the long run? We are taught that it had taken billions of years to evolve to this stage in our existence, so our brains and our bodies are probably near and or already perfect organic machines. Our bodies and brains are not stupid and I believe given the right conditions they can fix themselves. Being incarcerated in a stressful mental facility is not the right conditions.

I liken the brain to a computer. Years ago I remember fiddling around with the main processor in my PC. I had discovered from a mate Michael you could clock it (make it go faster) by altering the jumper settings on the main circuit board, I could then run more advanced software. It worked fine for a while but then I started to get errors or side effects, this is because I had made it do something it had not been designed to do. I believe that taking modern pharmaceutical drugs is having a similar effect on us, the same way as I clocked my PC. They all have side effects and simply get the mind and body doing things they are not designed to do, thus instead of solving a problem it causes others. These other problems or side effects then require additional medications to try and solve the errors caused but obviously they cannot because we as a species or model have probably already evolved or been designed to be as near as we are probably going to get to perfection. Coupled with the fact that as a result of us taking these drugs it happens to employ a lot of people and I mean a lot of people. I wonder if it is all being done on purpose and is a necessity of the way things have to be to lead the life we do.

I am now in the position where I have to take neuroleptic drugs every day, my brain has got used to the way they have changed the chemical balances within it. They have changed the natural workings of my body and I am now getting errors. I have put on 2 stone in weight and it's going up every month, I get tremors and blurred vision, my blood pressure is too high and I get diarrhoea. These are the things that are happening to me now; I dread to think what will be going on with my body 10 years from now. I have tried to stop taking neuroleptics like a lot of people do but the

Aaron

psychotic episodes I now get when off them are now so bad I cannot live with them. Doctors would say this is because I have stopped taking the medication a few times in the past or it is the natural progression of my illness which some say has progressed into schizophrenia. I disagree on both counts; I think the neuroleptics have damaged the way my brain works and made things irreversibly worse for me when I'm not taking them. I haven't got schizophrenia I am just sensitive to stress which causes me to see things some people cannot. I have been clocked, just like I clocked my computer all those years ago.

So what are we supposed to use instead of neuroleptic or antipsychotic drugs?

This is something the doctors should be thinking deeply about and not me, as I'm only a patient. These days the majority of young doctors think its best to take a pill when we become unwell, especially when it comes to problems with the mind. This may be because modern doctors have been trained to give out drugs in huge amounts especially when it comes to the old people, they have grown up in a world which is designed to have pharmaceuticals as a part of its culture or they just trust their peers are doing the right thing designing these medications as they consider it to be progress. Well it's definitely not progress; as I've already said I believe the body should be able to fix these problems, especially with the mind. All we have to do is find out the methods or situations we have to be in to allow it to accomplish this. This sounds hard but if we try and listen to our bodies and our minds they are probably telling us how to help fix things.

I have found things better after I have had natural sleep, it kind of resets everything in my head and I wake up feeling refreshed. When I cannot sleep, when I've been unwell I've tried sleeping tablets, alcohol, exercise and reading. Some of which sends me to sleep but I wake up in the same mind set as when I went to sleep. The best way I have found to get a good night sleep and feel better is spend the day in a non stressful environment and just lay there in a comfortable bed at night with the lights off trying not to think about anything. Sometimes I have laid there until the sun comes up but eventually I have gone to sleep and felt reset or refreshed when I have woken up. Another thing I have found helpful is to cry, there is a 10 year period in my life where I can't remember crying, within those ten years I would stop myself from crying because I was brought up in a culture where men shouldn't cry. If you feel like crying no matter where you are just cry because your mind is telling you that you need to. Another thing I feel is important is laughter, if you are in a situation where you feel like laughing out loads, you should just do it and don't worry what people think. I believe crying and laughing are important emotions which help to relieve stress on the mind and body and in my own experience has helped me sometimes to regain a manageable balance in my thoughts. Avoid stressful situations like work, driving in traffic and people that shout or are

Aaron

aggressive towards you. Just try and relax your mind and don't think about things too much. Don't do complicated tasks or get into deep conversations with doctors or psychotherapists as they tend to get you thinking about experiences which have happened to you in the past. Some of these experiences have probably made you unwell in the first place; you need to forget about them. You need to rest your mind and not overstress it or use it too much over a long period of time, just like you would a broken leg or arm.

I found while in Hospital that self occupational therapy has helped. Especially things that involve bright sunlight, nice smells and certain colours like whites, bright yellows and pastels. On a few occasions I sat outside in the summer making daisy chains on my own away from the noise and chaotic distractions of other patients which you sometimes get in group OT classes. I found this calming and away of focusing my attention on something that was not over demanding. It also smelt fragrantly nice and was pleasing to my eyes as I made them, this in the whole made me feel a lot better, although a bit poofy.

Natural Drugs

It is a common conception that natural recreational drugs like cannabis, cocaine or opium are worse than modern pharmaceutical drugs for the mind and body, after all modern drugs have been through stringent testing, they must be okay! I believe that cannabis, cocaine and opium in their mild natural forms not cloned or grown in hydroponics and taken in moderation are far better for us. We have been taking them for thousands of years, they have evolved or been designed with us. In my experience so far if I continue taking modern neuroleptic drugs I feel a lot more damage will be done to my mind and body in the long term than ever could be done with natural drugs. This is not a statement to promote the use of natural recreational drugs, my advice would be not to do them but I just wanted to highlight how I think modern pharmaceutical drugs are underrated at the damage they do to our minds and bodies. They are a very new thing and our minds and bodies are simply not use to them interfering with the workings of them.

So what do I think is wrong with me?

From reading parts of that book by Paul McKenna that Sam bought me 15 years ago. I have found out we actually have two main parts to our minds, a conscious and unconscious mind. The way Paul explains it is if you are in a room with a lot of people talking your unconscious mind is monitoring what everyone is saying. If someone over the other side of the room calls out your name your unconscious mind brings it to the attention of your conscious mind and you can hear them.

Well I believe bits of my conscious mind have been damaged through stress thus leaving me to have to operate with my unconscious mind at times. This is why I have had floods of thoughts, optical distortions and long moments of loss of concentration. I have in fact been flooded with information that is normally filtered out and past on to the conscious mind by the unconscious mind.

Although I have done a lot of recreational drugs in the past I don't believe this has had a significant impact on my illness. I say this because I first noticed myself getting ill in Thailand and I had not been taking any types of drugs for at least two years. The main cause of what happened to me was stress related as I believe most mental illnesses are. I then proceeded to get worse because of my environment back home in my country and at my families, also the taking of neuroleptic medication. Once I had been taking it coupled with my stressful environment it interfered with the natural attempts of the fixing of things by my body and mind and I become worse.

At the moment I am trying to get rid of and away from all stresses in my life. Once I have completed this I will try and come of the medication again and hope my mind and body is still capable of operating within its normally perimeters.

The NHS

The National Health Service is something I have spent a lot of time thinking about especially while under section in Hospital. Whilst in Hospital a nurse told me that the NHS is the largest employer in the country. I have just looked on the Internet and they employ directly over 1.3 million people and that's just in England and Wales. The NHS is in fact the third largest employer in the world! My worry here is because a lot of people are employed they are using sick people to create jobs or maybe even worse along with the pharmaceutical companies could be creating sick people to create jobs. I realise this sounds unbelievable especially when it come to the pharmaceutical companies but as I've said before all their drugs have side effects which require you to take more drugs in the future or even have surgery to correct the damage done. These drugs are expensive because they create a lot of well paid jobs. Could all this be being done on purpose I sometimes wonder and being disguised as progress. Could there not be something going on here?

As I'm writing this paragraph the NHS is celebrating its 60th birthday, the media is telling us on the news what a wonderful organisation it is and how we are the envy of the world. If it is such a great and moral thing to be giving out free medical care and drugs to everyone that wants it, then why is the media trying to sell it to us and why isn't the rest of the world doing it? The majority of people in this country including most of my family would think its because other countries are not clever enough to offer it but the fact is there is nothing clever with messing about with the natural workings of the mind and body, as I've already said in my opinion it can cause errors or side effects and above all it creates a lot of jobs;

after all our minds and bodies have been self governing themselves for millions of years and they should know what they are doing by now. Nothing in this world is for free and the ten years extra life we may get from participating in this pill popping and so called free medical care will cost us dearly. I don't mean just in people or money but just like taking any drug it could cost us our independence and freedom throughout our lives especially when we get into our old age.

What got me thinking about the NHS was I was under a section 3 at Canterbury, they wouldn't let me leave. I had refused to take medication for the reasons I have explained here in my story. An Occupational Therapist was trying to convince me to take it; she said she believed in medication. I asked her how many people were under section in Kent at the moment, she said she didn't know. I counted about 20 of us in Canterbury, 20 in Margate and probably another 20 at Ashford and what with the other hospitals probably around Kent I rounded it up to 200 of us. I thought to myself what would happen if they let us all go, apart from 200 hundred people acting what they consider to be mad or strange in the community. Well thousands of people would lose their jobs; they would all have nothing to do! I come to the conclusion that although some of them cared and were trying to help us there were in fact thousands of people from parts of the NHS all living of 200 of us being sectioned in Hospital. I then looked at the bigger picture and realised that the whole of the NHS including the pharmaceutical companies were doing the same thing but with the general population. From this point in my mind I come to the conclusion that it may be better for the medical industry to be on a casualty basis only as the temptation for them to create sick people to create jobs would be too great. Before this point I had assumed that other countries that don't have free medical care couldn't afford it or just simply were not governed properly as to be able to offer it; the fact is they simply don't need it. When they are seriously ill they have to pay money when they need hospital treatment or drugs; it's just about affordable for them and nothing like the insurance companies and the media would lead us to believe. This ensures they only go to hospital or doctors when it is necessary and creates a casualty type of health service like what we had before the 2nd world war and not an industrial type employment machine that lives off sick people. This is what I believe we may have today in the UK.

Aaron

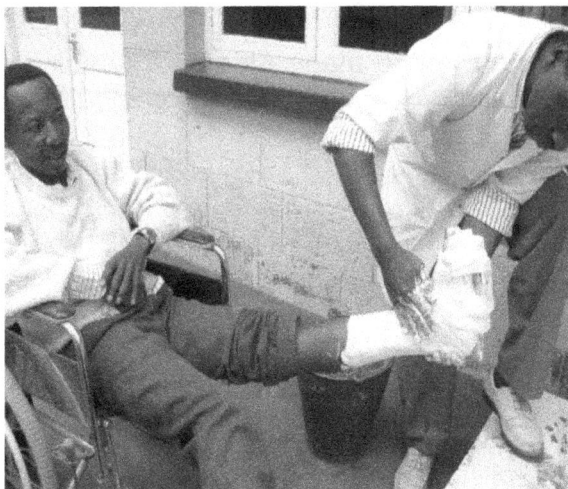

How it should be done: a man getting his foot plastered outside Arusha Hospital in Tanzania

I think it's possible the old people in this country and in most of the developed world are being used to create jobs for the working population. As soon as they have retired and completed their usefulness in working life the doctors have got them having blood tests. As a result of this they have put them on various assortments of pharmaceuticals, which as I've said previously are clocking them and causing all sorts of errors or side effects in their bodies. Our culture seems to be designed in this way and we think it's normal practise and it is but only in the developed world. In undeveloped or developing countries I have met a lot of old people over the years both expatriates and locals that have never taken a pill in their life, some of them have been in their late 80's and still getting about and going strong. In the UK the old people, in my opinion are being scared into thinking that these medications are keeping them alive and in some cases they are but only so they can be of use to the economy in creating jobs for the population i.e. the NHS machine and their suppliers, Nursing homes and pharmaceutical companies. I don't say the above lightly as it's something which really bothers me.

1996 Expatriate Lady in her 80's from Austria, Living in Bangalore, India since 1940

Aaron

I also wonder if the pharmaceutical companies who employ a lot of people in offices; as noticed while I worked at Pfizer's were to come up with a drug that cures every illness, would they actually use it? If they did use it then about 2 million people from them and the NHS would be out of a job and that's only the people directly employed by them. The knock on effect with suppliers like office supplies, food, uniforms and sub-contractors such as builders for new hospitals, offices and homes for nursing staff, hospital equipment and private consultants could be colossal. I'm guessing but maybe even in the region of 6 million people. That's about 21% of the working population of the UK. This could be why the doctors are being used in my opinion to mess with the workings of our minds and bodies and not leaving our brains to self regulate ourselves. I wonder if the only pill we indeed need to cure all illnesses is in fact just our minds.

Aerial view of Pfizers Office's in Sandwich, UK

Note to the readers

I actually started writing this as a personal thing, I was trying to recollect all the key moments in my life to help me understand what has gone wrong with me. I never intended it to be published at all until someone told me about Chipmunka Publishing. I thought other people may be interested in reading my story. My apology for the crude way of writing in some places but this is the first time I have written anything like this and at such length.

Thanks for reading my story.

Aaron ;)

www.ingramcontent.com/pod-product-compliance
Lightning Source LLC
Chambersburg PA
CBHW021158010426
R18062100001B/R180621PG41931CBX00019B/33